Catalogue of Australian Fossil Dragonflies

IAN ENDERSBY

First published by Busybird Publishing 2023

Copyright © 2023 Ian Endersby

ISBN:
Print: 978-1-922954-22-0

Cover design: Busybird Publishing

Layout and typesetting: Busybird Publishing

busybird
publishing

Busybird Publishing
2/118 Para Road
Montmorency, Victoria
Australia 3094
`www.busybird.com.au

Cover - QMF33409 © Australian Age of Dinosaurs, used with permission.

Frontispiece - Location of fossil dragonfly sites in Australia

Fossil Odonata Sites

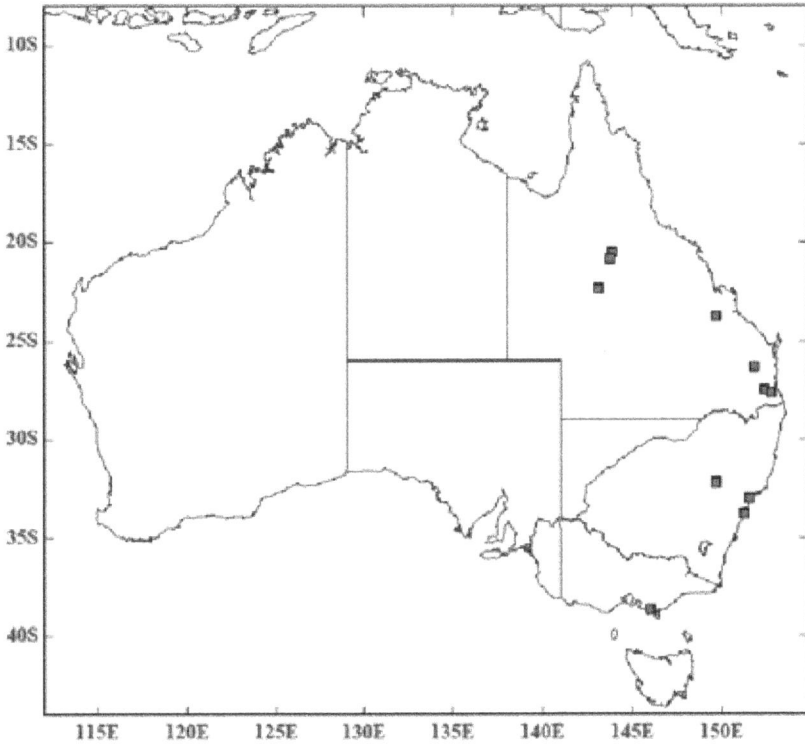

From north to south

Pelican Bore
Flinders River
Winton
Duaringa Core
Wondai
Brassall Quarry,
Denmark Hill, Mt Crosby, Dinmore Clay Pits
McGraths Flat
Talbragar Fish Bed
Warner's Bay, Beacon Hill
Koonwarra

Contents

Introduction   1
Fossil Families   7
Palaeomaps   11

The Fossils   19
     Aeschna flindersiensis (syn. Aeschnidiopsis flindersiensis)   19
     Aeschnidiopsis flindersiensis (1) holotype   22
     Aeschnidiopsis flindersiensis (2) Riek specimen   24
     Aeschnidiopsis flindersiensis (3) Pelican Bore   27
     Aeschnidiopsis flindersiensis (4) Winton   29
     Austrogomphus larvae   30
     Austroprotolindenia jurassica   31
     Coenagrionid indet. larvae   34
     Corduliidae indet. larvae   38
     Meganisoptera   39
     Mesophlebia antinodalis (1) Denmark Hill   41
     Mesophlebia antinodalis (2) Wondai   46
     Mesophlebia tillyardi (syn. Mesophlebia antinodalis)   47
     Niwratia elongata   49
     Peraphlebia tetrastichia   51
     Peraphlebia tetrastichia larvae   54
     Perrisophlebia multiseriata   57
     Polytaxineura stanleyi   59
     Samarura sp.   63
     Tillyardomyrmeleon petermilleri   65
     Triassagrion australiense   67
     Triassolestes epiophlebioides   72
     Triassophlebia stigmatica   75
     Not determined (AM display specimen F.39175)   78
     Not determined (Beacon Hill)   79
     Not Determined (Denmark Hill)   80
     Not Determined (Dinmore)   83
     Not Determined (Mount Crosby)   84
     Not Determined (Talbragar)   86
     Aeroplana mirabilis   Phasmodea   88
     Antitaxineura anomala   Plecoptera   91
     Austrolestidion duaringae   Decapoda: Parasticidae   93
     Mesomantidion queenslandicum   Protorthoptera   95

The Indexes   98
     Museum Holdings   98
     Fossils By Locality   102
     Holotype Repository   107

Acknowledgements   108
References   110

Introduction

It is a little over 100 years since Robin Tillyard named his first Australian dragonfly fossil (*Mesophlebia antinodalis* in 1916) although Australia's first fossil was *Aeschna flindersiensis* Woodward, 1884 which Tillyard renamed in 1917. Since then there have been major developments in wing vein nomenclature and in our knowledge of the phylogeny of the Odonata and their precursors.

Australian Museums, and the Natural History Museum in London, hold 61 dragonfly fossils from Australia, 32 as wings or wing fragments and 29 as larvae. Some have the part and counterpart preserved. The larvae total includes a specimen previously described as a flea. Also, four specimens initially described as Odonata are now recognised as belonging to different taxa.

Tierney et al. (2020) use the terminology "positive" and "negative" while most other authors, including Tillyard and Dunstan, refer to the two parts as "part" and "counterpart". It would appear that Dunstan retained the counterparts for his own personal collection so these became part of his estate which his widow sold to the British Museum (Natural History). This makes the listing of individual specimens difficult.

There are 27 counterparts so, if part and counterpart are counted separately, there are 89 specimens. [61 + 27 = 89 of which 8 (4 parts; 4 counterparts) are no longer recognised as dragonflies.]

Fossil Localities

Until the discovery of a Miocene deposit at McGraths Flat, New South Wales, bearing Odonata larvae, all Australian specimens were found in rocks of Late Permian or Mesozoic age, the Age of the Dinosaurs. The extent of those deposits can be seen in Figure 1.

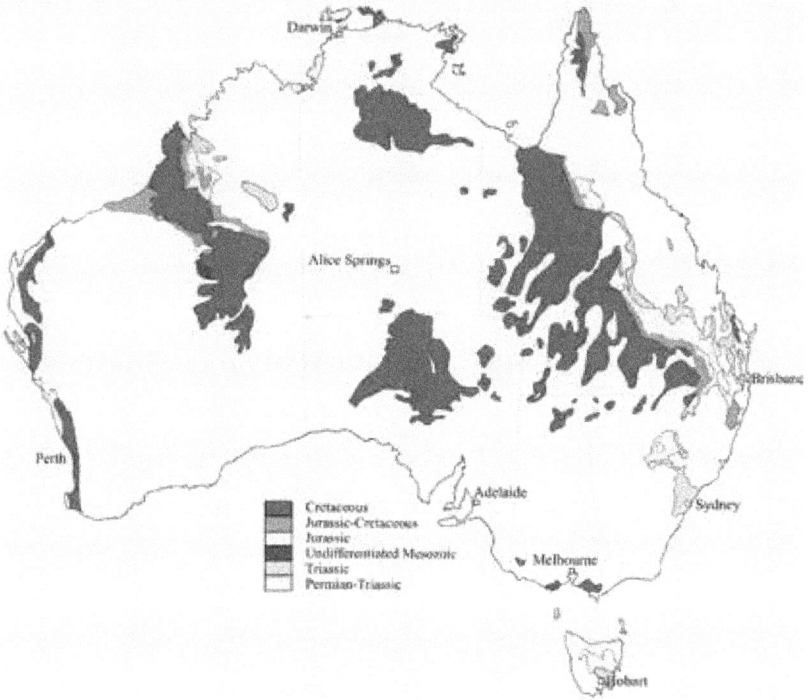

Figure 1 - Mesozoic Sediments of Australia

The location of most sites is shown in the frontispiece (p.iii) but the scale is not adequate to distinguish all localities. Those in the vicinity of Ipswich, Queensland can be seen in Figure 2.

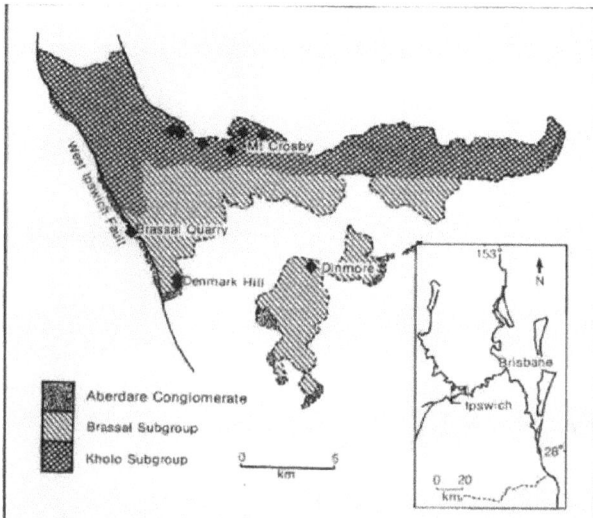

Figure 2 - Fossil Sites in the Vicinity of Ipswich, Queensland

An interesting news item in the *Bowen Independent* of 29 May 1936 p. 2 headed 'Search for Fossils' said "Dr. Tillyard's main purpose in visiting Bowen was to endeavour to find specimens of fossilized dragon flies, of which samples exist in an old continental museum labelled "Port Bowen" and "Port Denison". He had been requested to seek further specimens by the King of the Belgians, who is an enthusiastic collector. After an inspection of likely places locally however, the Doctor stated that no fossil insects exist here, and the mystery of those dragonflies remains unsolved."

This is pure speculation but the extant *Hemiphlebia mirabilis* was known as a living fossil as evidenced by Burns (1959) "Entomologists have come to recognize this insect as a 'living fossil' because of its archaic type of structure which shows direct affinities with fossil remains of dragon-flies in contrast with present-day forms", and its type locality was (erroneously) given as Port Denison which is the modern day Bowen. Perhaps this led to some confusion.

Although the King of the Belgians at that time was Leopold III, there is a history of palaeontological interest (Geoscientist Online Spring 2021 https://www.geolsoc.org.uk/Geoscientist/Archive/Dec-2018/Online-special).

In 1878, one of the greatest fossil dinosaur discoveries ever made was that of over 35 *Iguanodon* skeletons 322 m below ground in a Belgian coalmine. Realising their scientific importance, the miner's skills were diverted to recovering the skeletons, which were painstakingly reconstructed by the French-born palaeontologist Louis Dollo. Recognising the international importance of the find, the Belgian palaeontologists, with support from King Leopold II, cast the best-preserved skeleton. Replica casts were offered to the university museums of both Oxford and Cambridge, where they are still hold pride of place in the displays.

King Leopold II died without surviving legitimate sons. Subsequent Belgian kings descended from his nephew and successor, Albert I.

Benjamin Dunstan was appointed as Assistant Geologist to the Geological Survey of Queensland in 1897, promoted to Acting Queensland Government Geologist in July 1902, being confirmed in the position in 1908. He served as head of the Queensland Geological Survey until his retirement in January 1931. He and Robin Tillyard collaborated to document the late Triassic insects of Australia. Dunstan carefully curated and organised both the official government collection of these insects for the Geological Survey of Queensland, and his own private collection. Upon his death in 1933 his widow commenced to negotiate the sale of his large personal collection (including type and type counterpart specimens) to the British Museum. It took until the 1950s to finalise through his daughter.

Tillyard died in January 1937, aged 56, and his widow, Patricia, oversaw the disposal of his palaeontological collection, entrusting the assessment and sorting of it to the Australian Museum in Sydney. Mrs Tillyard wanted most of the Tillyard collection to go to the British Museum, as a donation rather than a sale; in addition, some material was donated to the Australian Museum. (Rix 2021, and references therein). Apparently Mrs Tillyard did not have legal title to the specimens to donate them to the AM, so they will be repatriated and will then revert to their QGS numbers (A.Rozefelds in litt.): *Mesophlebia antinodalis* (Figure 3), *Triassagrion australiense*(Figure 4); *Triassolestes epiphlebioides* (Figure 5); *Triassophlebia stigmata* (Figure 6).

Mesophlebia antinodalis F39270 (≡ GSQ127a), *Triassagrion australiense* F39253 (≡ GSQ290a); *Triassolestes epiphlebioides* F39266 (≡ GSQ205a); *Triassophlebia stigmata* F39267 (≡ GSQ82a)

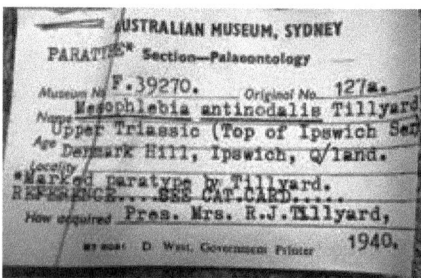

Figure 3

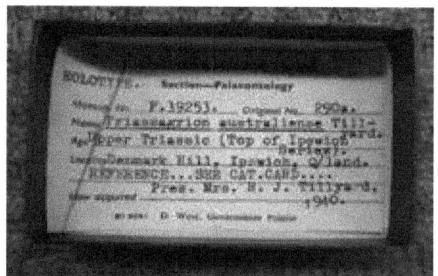

Figure 4

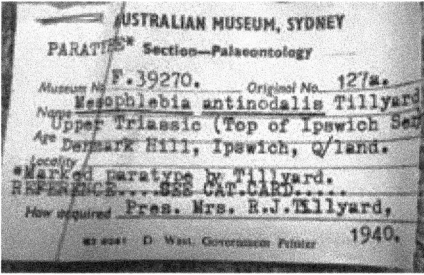

Figure 5

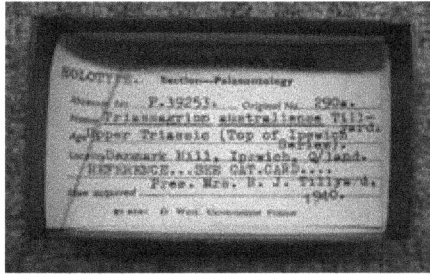

Figure 6

In the following table we can see which fossils at the London Natural Museum came from the estates of Tillyard and Dunstan.

Location	Prefix	Reg Number	Genus	Species	Gift from Tillyard Estate	Purchase from Dunstan Estate
WW 2.19	In	32925	Triassagrion	australiense		July 1935
WW 2.19	In	32972	Triassagrion	australiense		July 1935
WW 2.19	In	33126	Triassagrion	australiense		July 1935
WW 2.19	In	33226	Triassagrion	australiense		July 1935
WW 2.19	In	33279	Mesophlebia	antinodalis		July 1935
WW 2.19	In	33352	Triassophlebia	stigmatica		July 1935
WW 2.19	In	33397	Mesophlebia	antinodalis		July 1935
WW 2.19	In	33467	Perissophlebia	multiseriata		July 1935
WW 2.19	In	33469	Triassolestes	epiophlebioides		July 1935
WW 2.19	In	33519	Samaroblatta (?)	intercalata		July 1935
WW 2.19	In	33544	Triassagrion	australiense		July 1935
WW 7.23	In	33297	Austrolestidion	duaringae		July 1935
WW 2.22	In	33396	Aeroplana	mirabilis		July 1935
WW 2.19	In	33278	Mesomantidion	queenslandicum		July 1935
WW 2.7	In	45360	Polytaxineura	stanleyi	Oct. 1939 *	
WW 2.7	In	45781	Polytaxineura	stanleyi	Oct. 1939*	
WW 2.19	In	46112	Triassagrion	australiense	Oct. 1939	
WW 2.19	In	46116	Triassagrion	australiense	Oct. 1939	
WW 2.17	In	46119	Tillyardomyrmeleon	petermilleri	Oct. 1939	
WW 2.7	In	46392	Antitaxaneura	anomola	Oct. 1939	
WW 2.7	In	46395	Antitaxaneura	stanleyi	Oct. 1939	
WW 5.12	In	64602	Aeschnidiopsis	flindersiensis		

[1] *– these labels include "with aid of Roy. Soc. grant" [awarded in 1931]

Fossil Families

The Superorder Odonatoptera is one of the oldest insect groupings, with fossils known in the early Upper Carboniferous. It comprised three orders – †Geroptera; †Protodonata, noted for their gigantism and known colloquially as griffinflies; Odonata which contains all extant species. The group diversified during the Permian and the Triassic.

While representatives of the true Odonata are known in the Upper Permian, they diversified into Zygoptera and Epiproctophora (= Anisozygoptera + Anisoptera) during the Upper Triassic. The great development of the Anisoptera took place during the Jurassic. (Fleck & Nel, 2003). Thomas et al. (2013) declare "The split between the Odonata (dragonflies and damselflies), Ephemeroptera (mayflies), and Neoptera (the other winged orders) remains very much unresolved."

The original authors placed the species in the following familes but see footnotes for later opinions based on additional specimens and further analysis:

Aeschnidiopsis flindersiensis	Aeschnidiidae[2]
Austroprotolindenia jurassica	uncertain
Meganisoptera	Protodonata
Mesophlebia antinodalis	Mesophlebiidae[3] [4] [5]
Peraphlebia tetrastichia	Mesophlebiidae[6]
Perrisophlebia multiseriata	uncertain

---

2 - Fleck & Nel (2003) retain *Aeschnidiopsis flindersiensis* within Aeschnidiida -

3 - Nel & Paicheler (1994:330) declare "Comme ces fossiles ne sont que des moitiés apicales d'ailes, les structures des bases des ailes sont inconnues. ... Les Mesophlebiidae, famille baseé sur *M. antinodalis*, doivent être considérés comme des Odonata *incertae sedis.*" [As these fossils are only apical halves of wings, the base structures of the wings are unknown. ... The Mesophlebiidae family, based on *M. antinodalis*, must be considered as Odonata *incertae sedis.*]

4 - With the discovery and description of specimen QMF 58847 in Tierney et al. (2020) the family Mesophlebiidae is confirmed.

5 - Both Pritykina (1981) and Bechly (1997) synonymized Mesophlebiidae Tillyard, 1916 with Triassolestidae Tillyard, 1918.

6 - Nel & Paicheler (1994:331) "L'holotype de cette espèce n'a pas conservée caractères suffisants pour une détermination sure, même au niveau du sous-ordre. ... En consequence, cette aile ne peut être considéreé que comme un Anisoptera + Heterophlebioidea *incertae sedis.*" [The holotype of this species did not retain sufficient characters for a reliable determination, even at the suborder level. ... Consequently, this wing can only be considered as an Anisoptera + Heterophlebioidea *incertae sedis.*]

Polytaxineura stanleyi	Polytaxineuridae[7]
Samarura sp.	Zygoptera
Tillyardomyrmeleon petermilleri	Protomyrmeleontidae[8]
Triassagrion australiense	Protomyrmeleontidae[9]
Triassolestes epiophlebioides	Triassolestidae[10]
Triassophlebia stigmatica[11] [12]	

Nel et al (2002). "Tillyard (1922) described *Triassophlebia stigmatica* (Upper Triassic, Australia) and attributed it to the Mesophlebiidae. Nel et al. (1993) excluded it from this family and considered it as an Odonatoptera *incertae sedis*. Bechly (1997, p. 59) indicated that it 'could be a member of Parazygoptera'. We had the opportunity to re-examine the holotype specimen, In 33352, in the British Museum. This fossil is the apical part of a wing. If it has some very particular characters (e.g. IR_1 apparently branching on RP_2, a strong oblique cross-vein between RP_1 and IR_1 below pterostigma), none of the characters used as autapomorphies for the Parazygoptera Bechly, 1997 or any of the families of this clade is preserved in this fossil. Therefore, we prefer to maintain it as an *incertae sedis*."

There is much debate and little consensus about relationships of the Odonatoptera. With quite some licence, the table below represents the schema of Grimaldi & Engel (2005), after paying due homage to Fleck & Nel 2003; Huguet et al. 2002; Nel et al. 2002; Nel et al 2005; Nel et al 2017; Tierney et al. 2020; and numerous sites on the internet. Of *Perrisophlebia multiseriata*, Tillyard (1918) says "It is impossible to place this fragment definitely;" so no family is given.

---

7 - Huget et al, (2002) "Therefore, we exclude *P. stanleyi* from the Permaeschnidae and concur with the restoration of the family Polytaxineuridae by Bechly (1996). The exact relationship of this taxon within the Protanisoptera remains undetermined." and "The exact relationship of this taxon [*Polytaxineura stanleyi*] within the Protanisoptera remains undetermined."
8 - This species was described in 1997, after Zessin (1991) had monographed the family Protomyrmeleontidae.
9 - Zessin (1991: 101) retains this species within Protomyrmeleontidae.
10 - Nel et al. (2002) emend the diagnosis but retain this species in the family Triassolestidae.
11 - Tillyard (1922):"This new genus may be placed provisionally within the Mesophlebiidae, pending the discovery of more complete material.
12 - Nel & Paicheler (1994: 331) "Ce fossile n'a conservé aucun caractère qui permette de le rapprocher d'un groupe precis d'Odonatoptera. II est impossible de déterminer si l'aile était petiolée ou non. ... *Triassophlebia stigmatica* TILLYARD, 1922: *in* Odonata *incertae sedis*." [This fossil has not retained any character that allows it to be linked to a specific group of Odonatoptera. It is not possible to determine if the wing was petiolate or not. ... *Triassophlebia stigmatica* TILLYARD, 1922: *in* Odonata *incertae sedis*.]

Superorder Odonatoptera Martynov, 1932

    Order †Geroptera Petrulevicius and Gutiérrez 2016

    Clade Holodonata Grimaldi & Engel, 2005

        Order †Meganisoptera Martynov, 1932 (syn †Protodonata Brongniart, 1893)

        undescribed species from Warner's Bay, Belmont, NSW

    Order Odonata Fabricius, 1793

        Suborder †Protanisoptera Carpenter, 1931

            Family †Polytaxineuridae Tillyard 1935

            (subjective synonym of Permaeschnidae

            Martynov 1931 *fide* Carpenter (1992)

        Suborder †Archizygoptera Handlirsch, 1906 (syn Protozygoptera

        Tillyard, 1925)

            Family †Protomyrmeleontidae Handlirsch, 1906

            Tillyardomyrmeleon petermilleri Henrotay et al. 1997

            Triassagrion australiense Tillyard, 1922

        Suborder †Triadophlebioptera Bechly, 1996

        Suborder †Tarsophlebioptera Handlirsch, 1906

        Suborder Epiprocta Lohmann, 1996

            Infraorder Anisozygoptera Handlirsch, 1906 (syn

            Epiophlebioptera Tillyard, 1917)

            Infraorder Anisoptera Selys, 1854

                Family †Aeschniidae Needham, 1903

                Aeschnidiopsis flindersensis (Woodward, 1884)

                Family Corduliidae

                    corduliid indet

                Family Gomphidae

                    Austrogomphus sp.

                Family Protolindeniidae Handlirsch 1906

              Austroprotolindenia jurassica Beattie & Nel 2012.

        Suborder Zygoptera Selys, 1854

                Family †Triassolestidae Tillyard, 1918 (syn

                †Mesophlebiidae Tillyard, 1916

                Mesophlebia antinodalis Tillyard, 1916.

                Peraphlebia tetrastichia Jell & Duncan, 1986

                ?*Triassophlebia stigmatica* Tillyard, 1922

                Triassolestes epiophlebioides Tillyard, 1918

                    Samarura sp.

                Family Coenagrionidae

                    ?coenagrid indet from Koonwarra

Palaeomaps

The following Palaeomaps for each locality recognise movements due to plate tectonics since the time of deposition. They range from oldest to youngest and were produced using Gplates and are based on the Robinson Projection which was specifically created in an attempt to find a good compromise to the problem of readily showing the whole globe as a flat image. The Robinson projection was devised by Arthur H. Robinson in 1963 in response to an appeal from the Rand McNally company, which has used the projection in general-purpose world maps since that time. Robinson published details of the projection's construction in 1974. The National Geographic Society (NGS) began using the Robinson projection for general-purpose world maps in 1988, replacing the Van der Grinten projection.

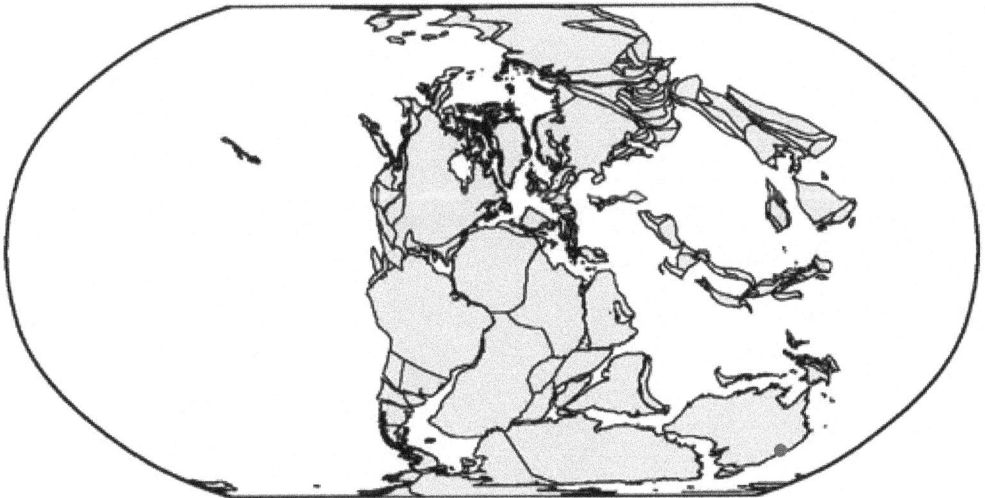

250 Mya - Warner's Bay, Belmont, NSW

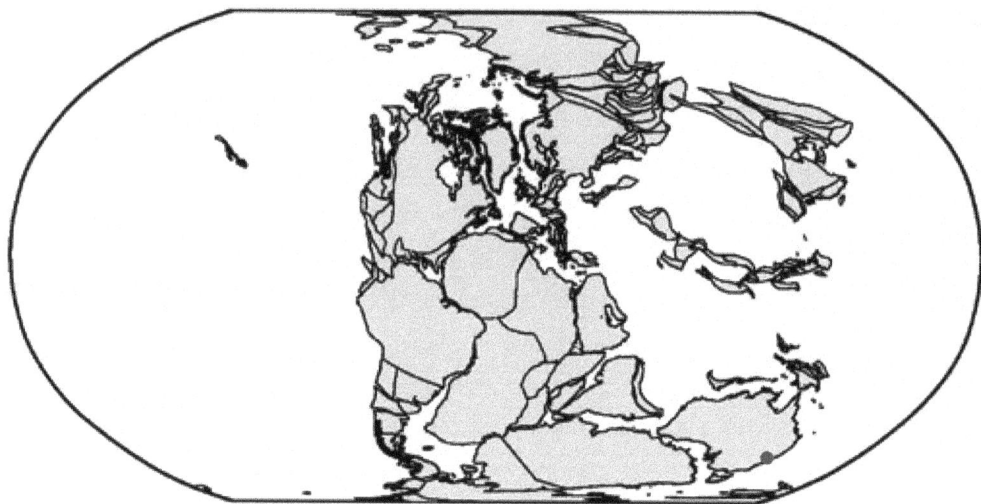

240 Mya - Beacon Hill, Brookvale, NSW

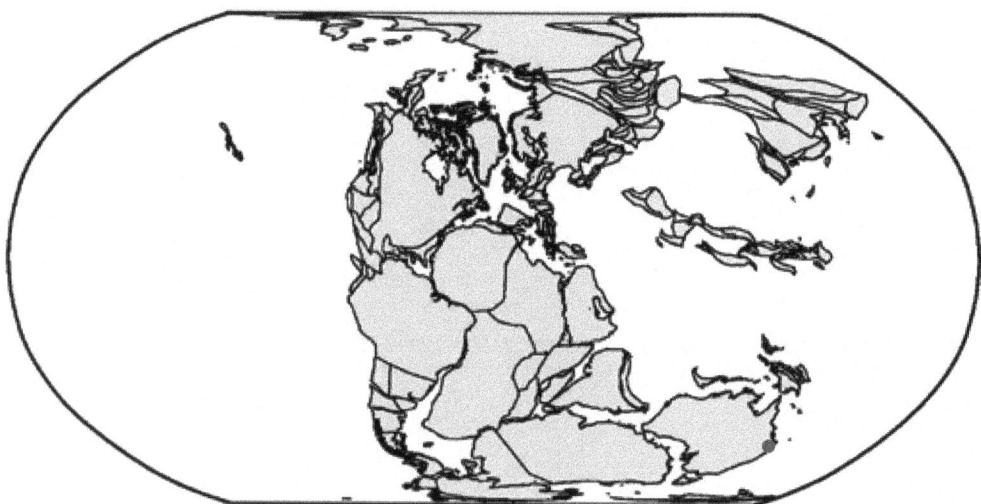

225 Mya - Wondai, QLD

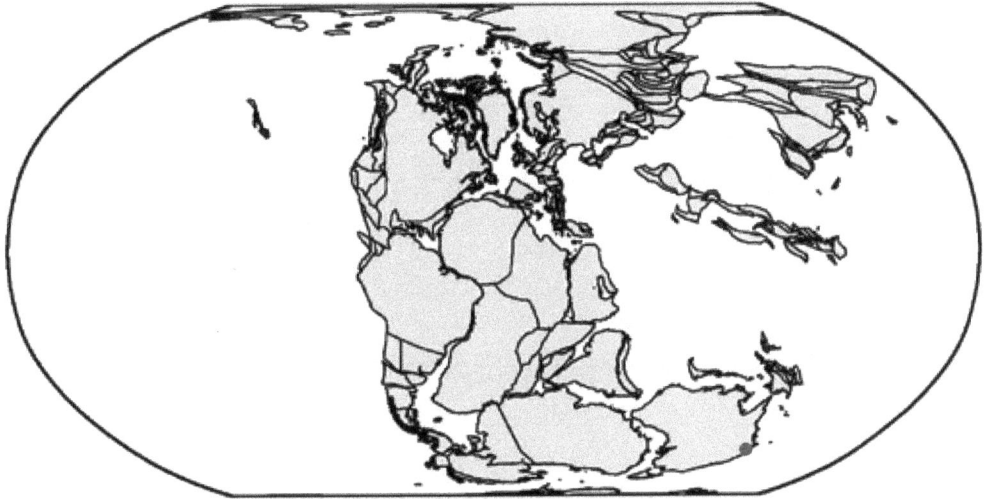

215 Mya - Denmark Hill Insect Bed, QLD - Mount Crosby Insect Bed, QLD

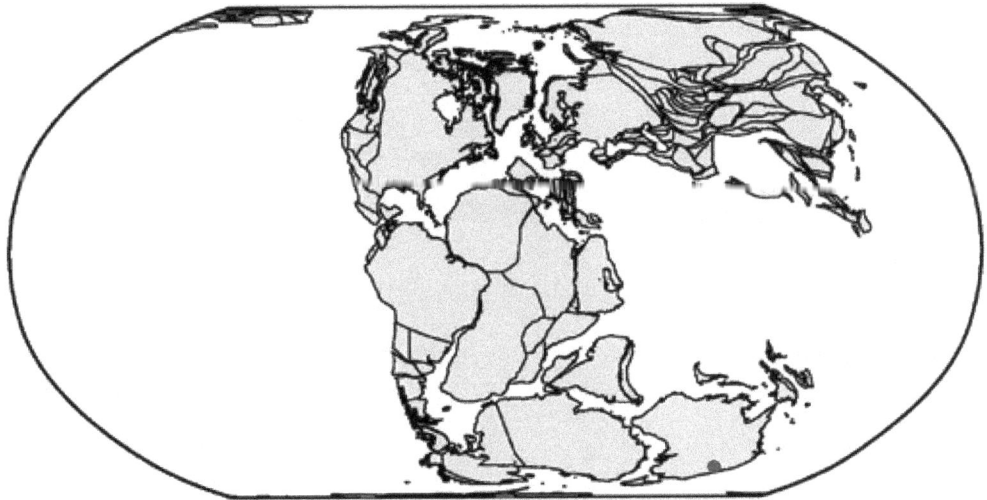

155 Mya - Talbragar Fossil Fish Bed, NSW

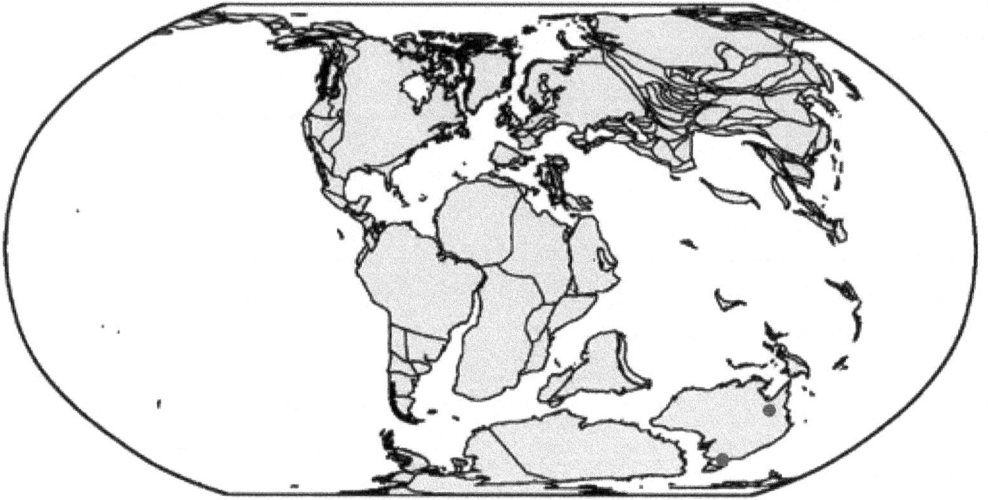

120 Mya - Flinders River Beds, QLD - Koonawarra Fossil Bed, VIC

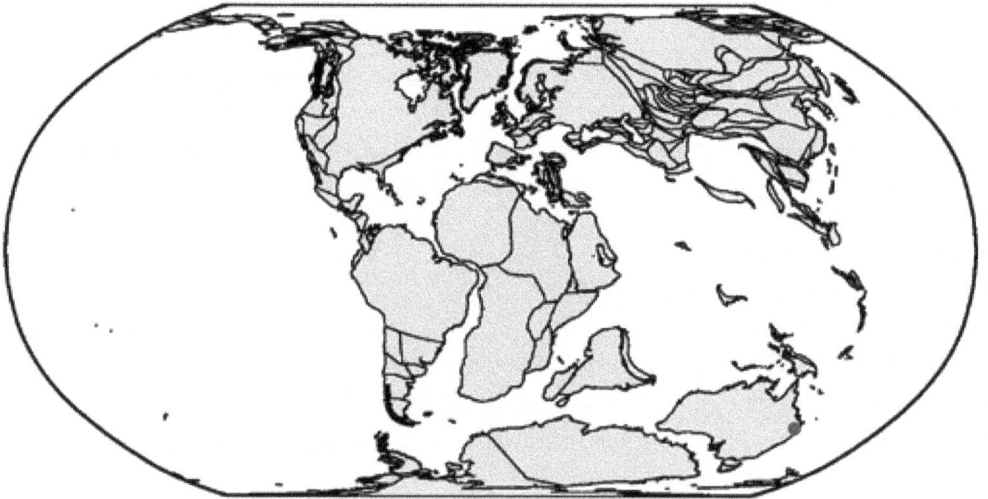

115 Mya - Brassall Quarry, QLD

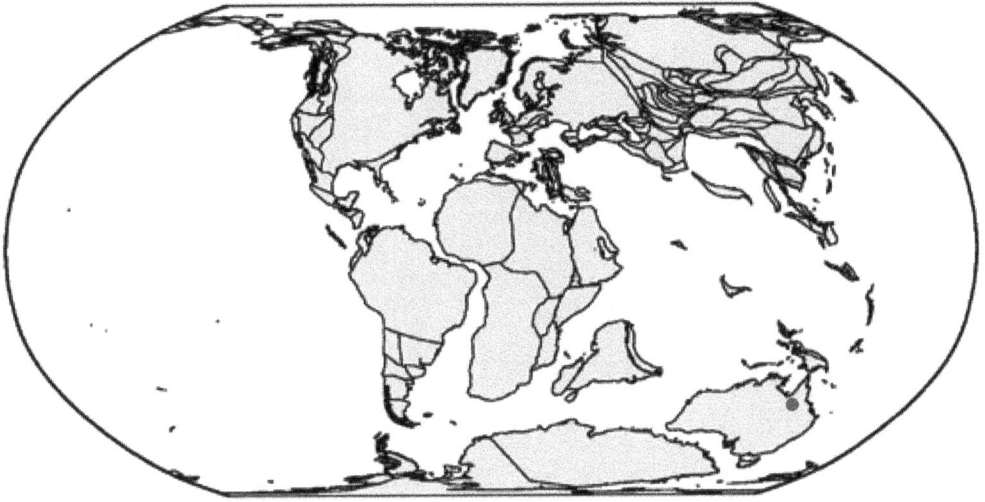

110 Mya - Pelican Bore, QLD

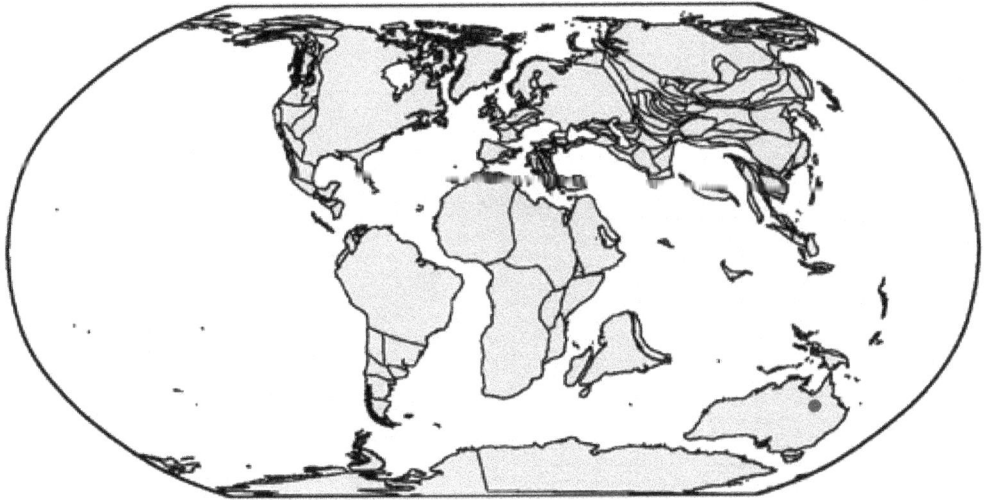

93 Mya - Winton, QLD

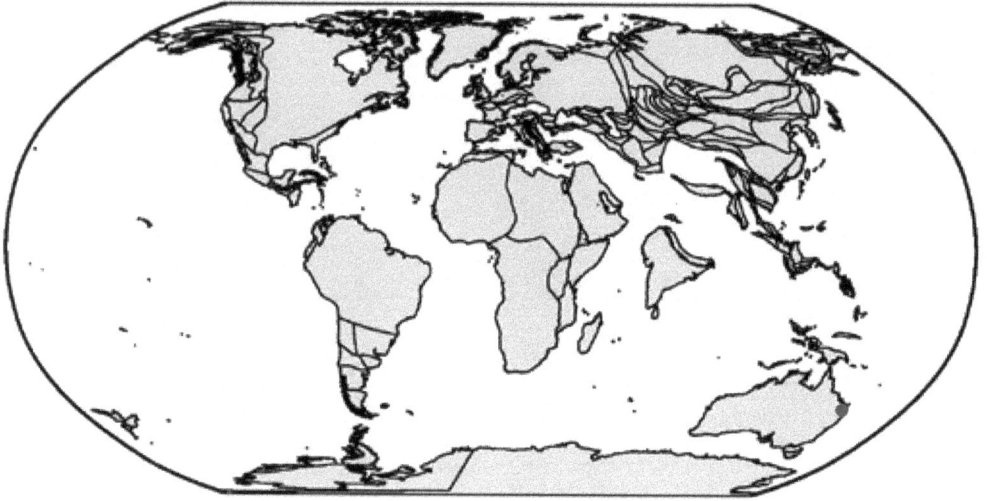

55 Mya - Dinmore Clay Pit, QLD

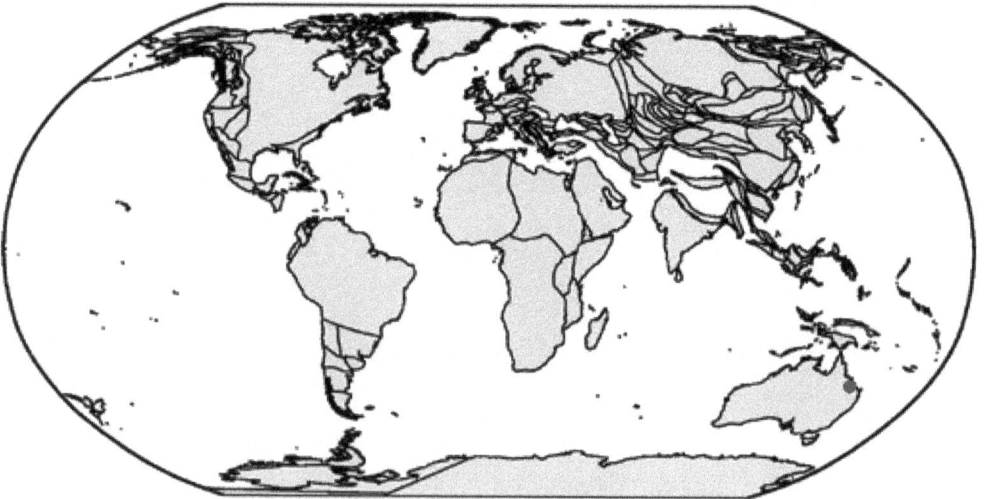

35 Mya - Duaranga Core, QLD

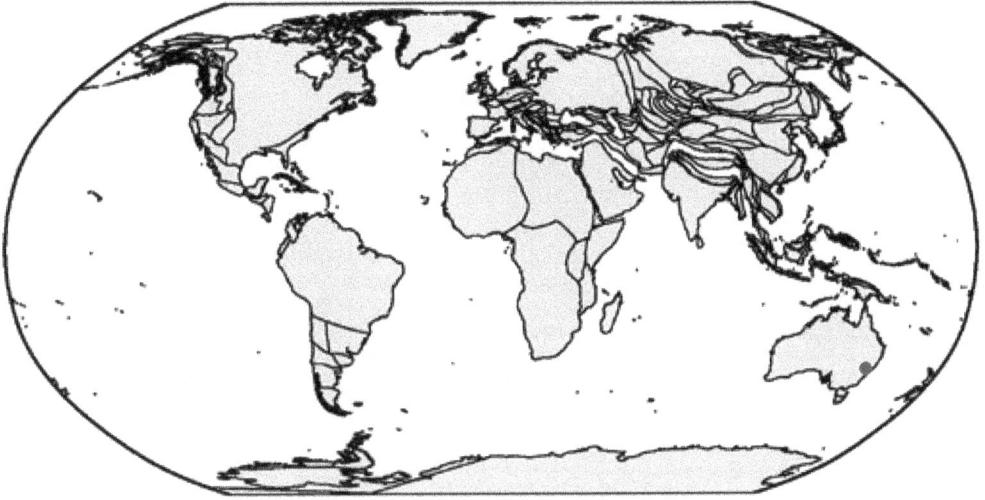

13 Mya - McGraths Flat, NSW

The Fossils

Aeschna flindersiensis Woodward, 1884

Family	Aeschnidioidea
Repository	Queensland Museum
Registration Number(s)	Queensland Geological Survey #368

Original description

Woodward, H. (1884). On the wing of a neuropterous insect from the Cretaceous limestone of Flinders River, north Queensland, Australia. *Geological Magazine, Decade III* 1:337-339 [Pl.XI Fig. 1]

Etymology of species name

A toponym from its type locality – Flinders [River] +*–ensis –is –e* = L. adjectival suffix indicating place of origin.

Locality	Flinders River, QLD
Geocordinates	20.8° S, 143.7° E
Palaeocoordinates	53.1° S, 122.7° E

Collector and Date

Jack, R.L. (1886) – "In accompanying the Transcontinental Railway Expedition, in 1881-2, I made a collection of fossils from the Rolling Downs, which was sent to London. I am indebted to Dr. Henry Woodward for a description of a new neuropterous insect [*Geological Magazine*, New Series, Decade 3, vol. 1, p. 337] … "

Dunstan's GSQ label #386 (Figure 7) adds "Rolling Downs 7 miles above Marathon Stn. Flinders River".

Stratigraphic Information (from Paleobiology Database)

The rock-specimen, on which a number of fragments of *Aucella* [*Aucella* is a genus of clams characteristically found as fossils in marine rocks of the Jurassic Period (between about 176 million and 146 million years old)] are plainly visible, is hard, dark greyish-brown and moderately fine grained.

Geological Age   Early Cretaceous: Aptian

Age MYA   125.0 ± 1.0 Ma to 113.0 ± 1.0 Ma

Voucher Number from Original Description

Tillyard 1917 "Type in Coll. Queensland Geol. Survey, Brisbane, Q."

Comments

Recombined as *Aeschnidiopsis flindersiensis* by Tillyard (1917) [see next entry].

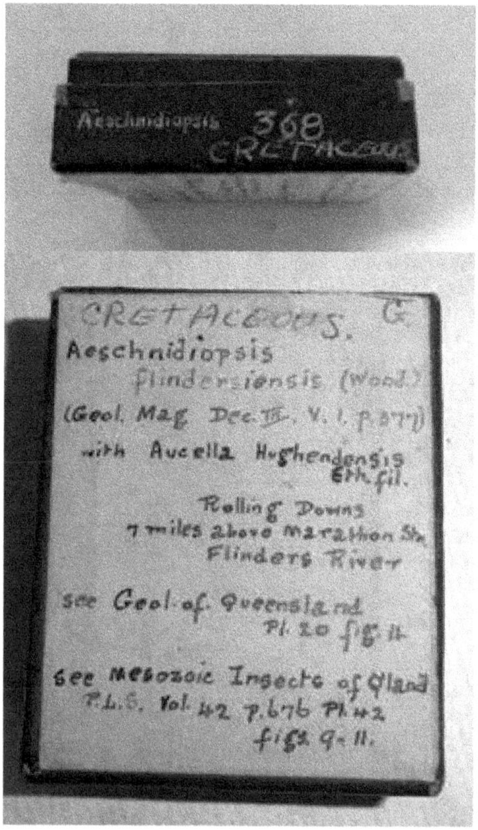

Figure 7 - Original Geological Survey of Queensland storage used by Benjamin Dunstan

Figure 8 - Woodward specimen (holotype)

Aeschnidiopsis flindersiensis (Tillyard, 1917)

Family	Aeschnidioidea
Repository	Queensland Museum
Registration Number(s)	Dunstan Collection #368
Original description	

Tillyard, R. J. (1917). Mesozoic Insects of Queensland no. 2 The fossil dragonfly *Aeschnidiopsis* (*Aeschna*) *flindersiensis* Woodward, from the Rolling Downs (Cretaceous) Series. *The Proceedings of the Linnean Society of New South Wales* **42**: 676-692 [pls. xlii, xliii]

Etymology of Genus name

Aeschnid + Gr. ὄψις= appearance, used as a suffix to denote resemblance.

Locality - Eromanga Basin: Wallumbilla Formation (Poropat in litt.) : 7 miles N of Marathon Station, Richmond, QLD, Flinders River Beds, QLD also called "Rolling Downs".

"The locality is not far from the town of Hughenden, and is now classed as Western Queensland; it lies almost exactly half-way along a North-South line drawn from Cape York to the New South Wales border." [footnote p. 676 of Tillyard (1917)]

Geocordinates	20.8° S, 143.7° E
Palaeocoordinates	60.2° S, 124.4° E
Stratigraphic Information (from Paleobiology Database)	

The rock-specimen, on which a number of fragments of *Aucella* [*Aucella* is a genus of clams characteristically found as fossils in marine rocks of the Jurassic Period (between about 176 million and 146 million years old)].are plainly visible, is hard, dark greyish-brown and moderately fine grained.

Geological Age	Early Cretaceous: Aptian
Age MYA	125.0 ± 1.0 Ma to 113.0 ± 1.0 Ma
Other References	Handlirsch A. (1908)

Voucher Number from Original Description

Tillyard 1917 "Type in Coll. Queensland Geol. Survey, Brisbane, Q."

Comments

Tillyard (1917: 676-677) "Wishing to study this insect, I wrote some years ago to the Director of the Queensland Museum, to try to find its whereabouts. He soon satisfied me that it was not in the Museum Collection. Inquiries from Mr. Dunstan, Chief Government Geologist of Queensland, at the Geological Survey, elicited the fact that nothing was known of it there. I wrote, therefore, to the British Museum authorities for information, and was informed that the fossil had undoubtedly had been returned by Dr. Woodward to the Queensland Geological Survey Collection; where it was ultimately found, without a label, in an accumulation of old specimens."

Fleck G., Nel A. (2003 51) provide a revised diagnosis because "There are several strong errors in the redescription proposed by Tillyard (1917) ... Tillyard (1917) indicated that the ScP of *Aeschnidiopsis* was ending in the nodus. Nel & Martínez-Delclos (1993) put in doubt this reconstruction. After the direct re-examination of the holotype, it appears that ScP is coming through the nodus as in other Aeschniidae".

Aeschnidiopsis flindersiensis (Tillyard, 1917)

Description

> Riek, E. F. (1954) A second specimen of the dragon-fly
> *Aeschnidiopsis flindersiensis* (Woodward) from the Queensland
> Cretaceous. *The Proceedings of the Linnean Society of New South
> Wales* **79**: 61-62

Repository   Queensland Museum

Registration Number(s) UQF.3162 Geology Department, University of
Queensland. Transferred to Queensland Museum in 1999.
QMF.2421 counterpart – confirmed by QM staff putting them in
juxtaposition'

Locality - Flinders River Beds, QLD also called "Rolling Downs". [but see
previous entry]. From Museum label: "Stewart's Creek, near ~~Hughenden~~
Richmond Q. [QM Fossil Register n.d. but between 1934 and 1936]".
Geocordinates 20.8° S, 143.7° E
Collector and Date

> C. Ogilvie, March 12, 1934 [QM Fossil Register No. 1 063

Voucher Information from Description

> Riek (1954: 61) "A second hindwing of this species is in
> the Collection of the Geology Department, University of
> Queensland (F.3162)"

Comments

> "Alex Cook (pers. comm.) stated that this specimen derived
> from the Toolebuc Formation, not the Doncaster Member of
> the Wallumbilla Formation (Poropat in litt.) [contra Jell (2004)
> who stated this fossil came from the Wallumbilla Formation.]

> Fleck G.& Nel A. (2003:51) "Nel & Martínez-Delclos
> (1993) note that the specimen F.3162 (Collection of Geology
> department, University of Queensland, Australia, same outcrop)

described and attributed to A. *flindersiensis* by Riek (1954) probably belongs to another genus and species. After the present redescription of *A. flindersiensis* we conclude that is the case, on the basis of the presence of infrasubdiscoidal cells in the specimen described by Riek (1954)."

"Charlie Ogilvie was a legendary figure in the [Irrigation and Water Supply] Commission by the 1930s. Appointed in 1913 as a hydraulic surveyor, he later graduated in electrical engineering. After serving in World War I as a musician, he joined the Commission. The mathematics of ground water was a relatively new discipline in the 1930s, previous analysis having been based on heat and electricity flow. Charlie Ogilvie was an early pioneer who took charge of the mathematical side of the analysis of the Great Artesian Basin. Ogilvie designed the Mt Isa dam for Mt Isa Mines without the Commission's knowledge, while he was District Engineer in Winton." {Watery Sauces : Water Resources Retirees' Association Inc. (2010) pp.32, 33

Nel, A. & Martínez-Delclòs, X. (1993: 49) "Il apparaît que le type de cette espèce différerait sensiblement du specimen étudié par RIEK, si nous considérons les descriptions par TILLYARD et de RIEK comme fiables. Les structures des espaces sous-discoïdaux et des champs cubito-anaux sont en particulier très nettement différentes et pourraient suffire à attribuer ces fossiles à des genres different. Ces deux fossiles mériteraint une revision détaillée avant d'être vraiment utilizable pour une etude phylogénétique que de cette familie.

"L'examin critique de ces descriptions des specimens d'une des espèces d'Aeschninidiidae le mieux connues [FRASER (1957) l'a choisie comme exemple typique de cette famille] montre bien j'usqu'à quell point les renseignements existants sur ces animaux sont incomplets, imprecise et peu cohérents." [[It would appear that the type of this species would differ significantly from the specimen studied by RIEK, if we consider the descriptions by TILLYARD and RIEK to be reliable. The structures of the sub-discoidal spaces and the cubital-anal fields are in particular very clearly different and could be sufficient to attribute these fossils to different genera. These two fossils deserve a detailed review before they are really useful for a phylogenetic study of this family.

Critical examination of these descriptions of specimens of one of the best-known species of Aeschninidiidae [FRASER (1957) chose it as a typical example of this family] shows how well the existing information on these animals is incomplete, imprecise and inconsistent.]

Figure 9 - UQF. 3162

Figure 10 - QMF. 2421

Aeschnidiopsis flindersiensis (Tillyard, 1917)

Repository	Natural History Museum	Queensland Museum
Registration Number(s)	In 64602	QMF.12035 counterpart

Locality - Pelican Bore, Stewart Creek, Dunhaven Homestead 55m NNW of Hughenden QLD

Geocordinates	20.535° S, 143.984° E
Palaeocoordinates	51.7° S, 130.0° E
Collector and Date	

QM-London University-BM(NH) expedition to Richmond and Hughenden; 1978

Geological Age	Late Albian
Age MYA	113 – 100.5
Comments	

Mather (1986) "In 1978 Wade, Thulborn and Bartholomai joined a British Museum (Natural History) expedition to Queensland to collect Mesozoic reptiles. Most of the important specimens from this expedition are being prepared in London and then will be returned to the Queensland Museum. An exception was the dragonfly wing from the Cretaceous which was retained in Queensland—a wing of the same age and possibly the same family as that acquired by the museum in the 1920s [probably QMF.2421]".

Figure 11 - In 64602

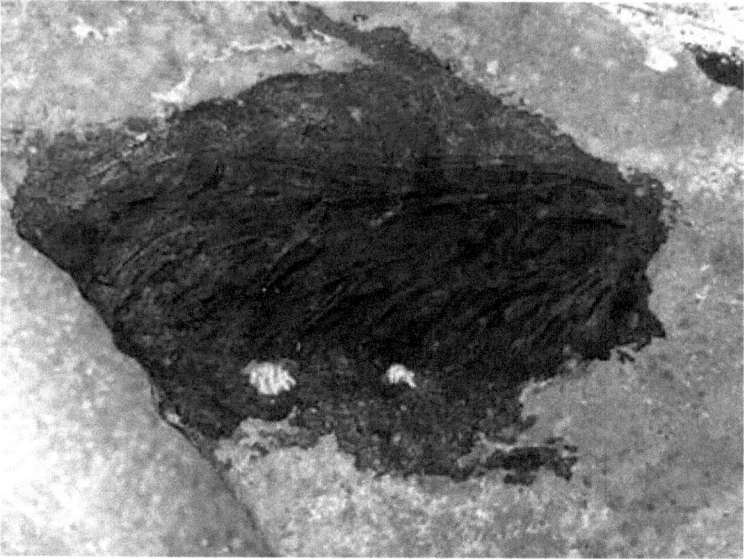

Figure 12 - QMF.12035

Figure 13 - QMF33409 © Australian Age of Dinosaurs, used with permission.

Aeschnidiopsis flindersiensis Tillyard, 1917

Repository	Queensland Museum
Registration Number(s)	QMF44309 part and counterpart

Description

    Elliott, D. & Cook. A. (2004).

Locality - Middle South Dam Excavation (in wall). Belmont Station, NE of Winton, Central West Queensland [locality number AODL0015]

Geocordinates Because the locality is on private property, the coordinates are confidential 22.3° S, 143.1° E (see Comments below)

Palaeocoordinates	52.3° S, 138.3° E
Collector and Date	David & Judy Elliott; March 2003
Stratigraphic Information	

    Winton Formation, Cretaceous

Geological Age	Cenomanian to Turonian
Age Ma	99.7 - 89.3
Comments	

Coordinates and Age based on Ho-Hum site, Belmont Station which is in the public domain

Elliot & Cook (2004) "During excavations to collect sauropod dinosaurs in the Upper Cretaceous, fluviatile, nonmarine Winton Formation near Winton, western Queensland, three insect specimens have been collected. One is a dragonfly wing, the same or similar to that from the marine Walumbilla Formation" (Jell 2004)

Elliott & Cook (2004) include a photo and attribute the specimen to *Aeschnidiopsis flindersiensis*

Austrogomphus sp.

Supplementary Table S1 of McCurry et al (2022) records 3 specimens of this taxon determined by Professor Victor Barinov. They have not yet (January 2023) been registered by the Australian Museum which will be their ultimate repository

Family   Gomphidae
Reference

> McCurry, M.R., Cantrill, D.J., Smith, P.M., Beattie, R., Dettmann, M. Baranov, V., Magee, C., Nguyen. J.M.T., Forster, M.A., Hinde. J., Pogson, R., Wang, H., Marjo, C.E., Vasconcelos, P. & Michael Frese, M. (2022). A Lagerstätte from Australia provides insight into the nature of Miocene mesic ecosystems. *Science Advances* 8 eabm 1406, 07 Jan 2022: 11 pp.

Locality - Mc Graths Flat ~25 km northeast of Gulgong, NSW
Geocordinates   32.1° S; 149.7° E because the deposit is on
                       private property only approximate coordinates
                       are given to preserve confidentiality.

Palaeocoordinates   40.08° S; 149.8° E
Stratigraphic Information from McCurry et al (2022)
      "similar to an oxbow lake".
Geological Age   early to middle Miocene
Age Mya   ~ 11 - 16

Austroprotolindenia jurassica Beattie & Nel, 2012

Family   Protolindeniidae

Repository   Australian Museum

Registration Number(s) - F.136868 and counterpart F.13869; Second specimen F. 141097 [part] & F. 141098 [counterpart] (Nel et al. 2017)

Original description

> Beattie, R. G. & Nel, A. (2012). A new dragonfly, *Austroprotolindenia jurassica* (Odonata: Anisoptera), from the Upper Jurassic of Australia. *Alcheringa* **36**:189-193. [pp. 2-3; figs. 1, 2]

Etymology of genus name

> Beattie & Nel (2012) "Genus named after Australia and the rather similar Jurassic genus Protolindenia, gender feminine." *Protolindenia* (≈ first Lindenia) refers to the recent gomphid genus *Lindenia* named after the Belgian entomologist P.L. Vanderlinden (1797-1831), which it seemed to precede.

Etymology of species name

> Beattie & Nel (2012) "Species named after the Jurassic age of the fossil."

Locality - Surat Basin: Purlawaugh Formation:Talbragar Fossil Fish Bed, Farr's Hill, NSW

Geocordinates   32.2° S, 149.7° E

Palaeocoordinates   72.6° S, 83.2° E

Collector and Date

> Beattie & Nel (2012) "The fossil was collected from the Talbragar Fossil Fish Bed in 2010".

Stratigraphic Information (from Paleobiology Database)

> The deposit represents a remnant of sedimentary accumulation in a freshwater lake. Sediment is largely derived from consolidated volcanic ash.

Geological Age

Late Jurassic: Latest Oxfordian-Tithonian, or early Tithonian.

> Although previously regarded to be of Early Jurassic age (Hind & Helby 1969), a latest Oxfordian–Tithonian (Late Jurassic) age has recently been determined by SHRIMP analysis of zircon crystals obtained from this unit (Bean 2006).

Age MYA: 151.55 +/- 4.27 Ma (error bar falls within Kimmeridgian).

Other References

> Beattie, R.G. & Avery, S. (2012). Palaeoecology and palaeoenvironment of the Jurassic Talbragar Fossil Fish Bed, Gulgong, New South Wales, Australia, *Alcheringa* 36: 453-468
>
> Nel, A., Frese, M., McLean, G. & Beattie, R. (2017). A forewing of the Jurassic dragonfly *Austroprotolindenia jurassica* Beattie & Nel (Odonata: Anisoptera) from the Talbragar Fish Bed, New South Wales, Australia, *Alcheringa*: **41**, 532-535 [Fig 8C].

Comments

> Nel et al. (2017)"Holotype a hindwing superimposed on a forewing."

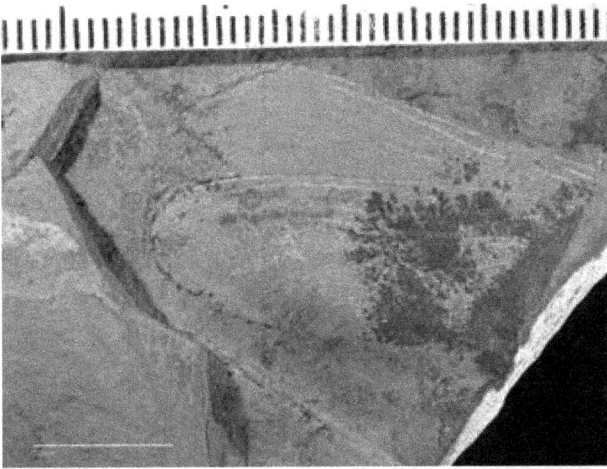

Figure 14 - F.136868

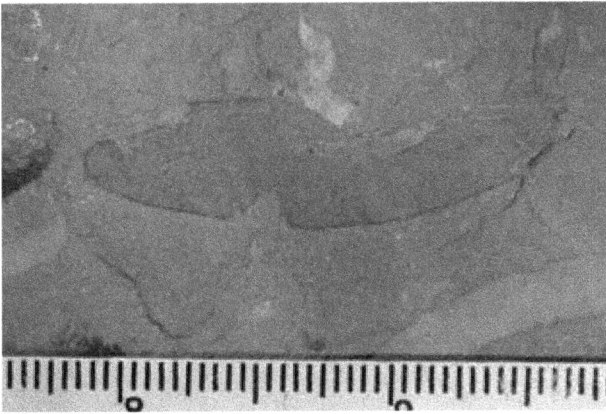

Figure 15 - F13869
counterpart

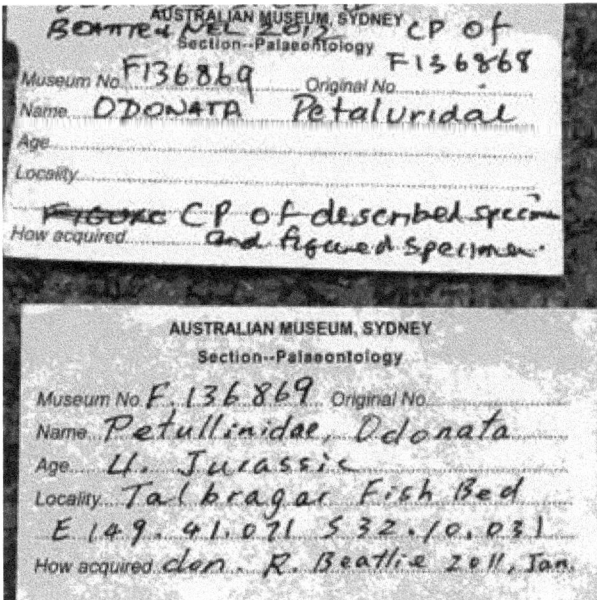

Figure 16 - AM Labels

Coenagrionidae indet. determined by Jell and Duncan (1986)

Repository   National Museum of Victoria

Registration Number(s) [Figure numbers from Jell & Duncan (1986)]

NMVP 102508 mature larva - Fig12 A,B,C

NMVP 102509 larva - Fig 12F

NMVP 103019 immature larva - Fig 12D

NMVP 102510; NMVP 103047; NMVP 103211

NMVP123054 [previously MUGD 3738] larva - Fig 12G

NMVP 27039

Description

Jell, P. A. & Duncan, P. M. (1986). Invertebrates, mainly insects, from the freshwater, Lower Cretaceous, Koonwarra Fossil Bed (Korumburra Group), South Gippsland, Victoria. *Memoirs of the Association of Australasian Palaeontologists* **3**:111-205. [pp. 126-131; figs. 8-10]

Locality - Koonwarra Fossil Bed, VIC NMVPL425

Geocordinates   38.6° S, 146.0° E

Palaeocoordinates   77.0° S, 118.6° E

Geological Age   Cretaceous: Late Aptian

Stratigraphic Information (from Paleobiology Database)

The Koonwarra Fossil Bed of South Gippsland, Australia, is =8 m thick, and the invertebrate fossils occur mainly on the lower strata just above an apatite layer dated 118 ± 5 million yr old and below a layer dated 115 ± 5 million yr old (Drinnan & Chambers 1986, Jell & Duncan 1986). Orig. assigned to Korumburra Group.

Numerous aquatic and semiaquatic insects in this bed, and the finely stratified mudstone that contains them, indicate a shallow pond with marshy edges that received periodic muddy influx from a larger adjacent lake.

Age Mya   122.46 to 112.6 Ma

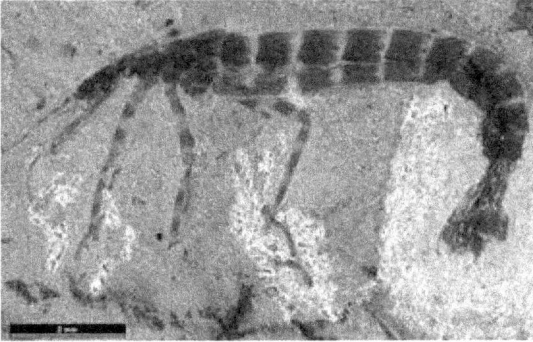

Figure 17 - NMV P123054 (previously MUGD 3738)

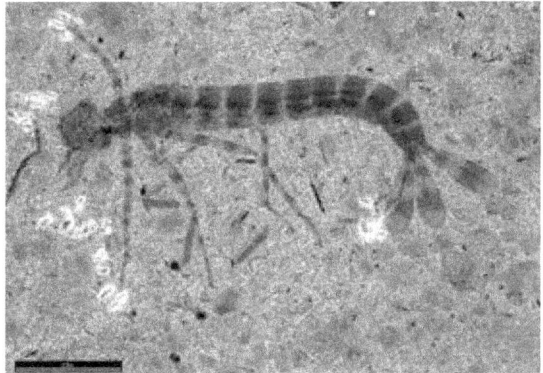

Figure 18 - NMV P102508A (part)

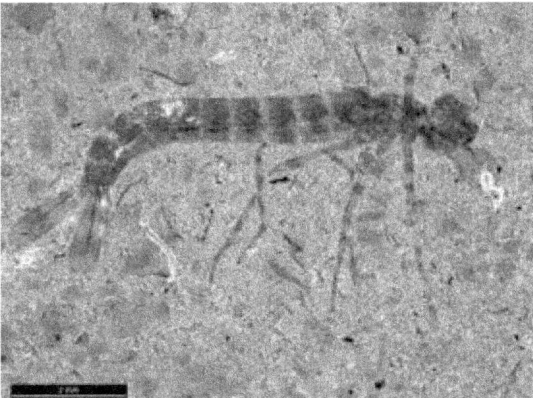

Figure 19 - NMV P102508B (counterpart)

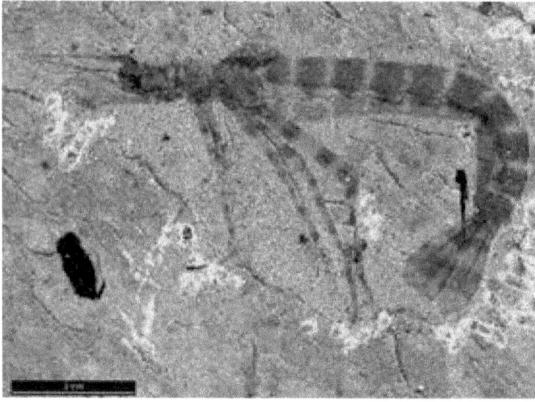

Figure 20 - NMV P102509A (part)

Figure 21 - NMV P102509B (counterpart)

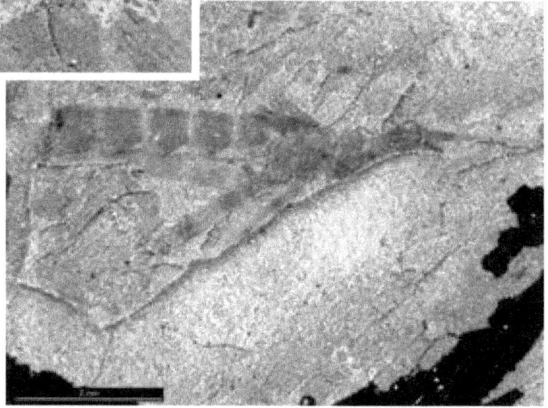

Figure 22 - NMV P102510

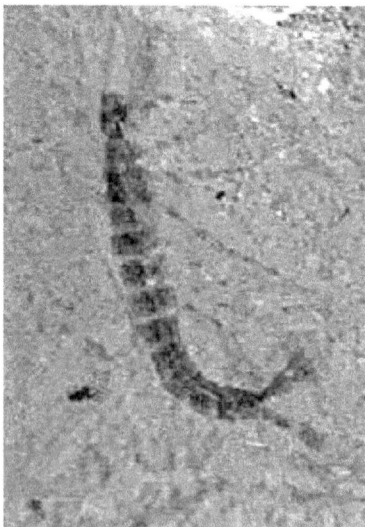

Figure 23 - NMV P103019

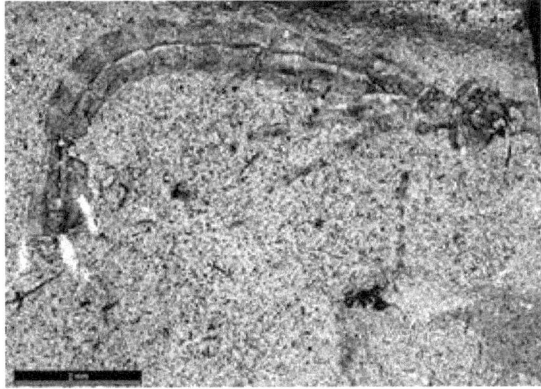

Figure 24 - NMV P103047

Figure 25 - NMV P103211

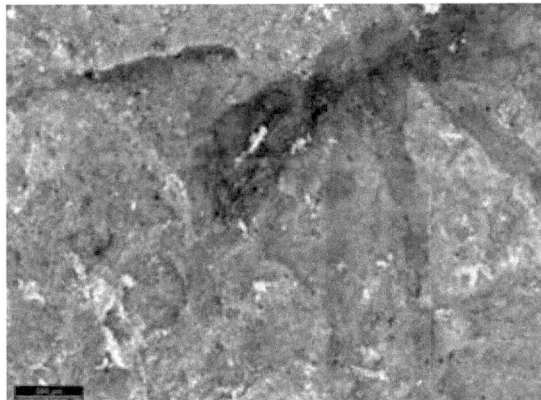

Figure 26 - NMV P27039

Corduliidae indet.

Supplementary Table S1 of McCurry et al (2022) records 13 specimens of this taxon determined by Professor Victor Barinov. They have not yet (January 2023) been registered by the Australian Museum which will be their ultimate repository

Family   Corduliidae

Reference

> McCurry, M.R., Cantrill, D.J., Smith, P.M., Beattie, R., Dettmann, M. Baranov, V., Magee, C., Nguyen. J.M.T., Forster, M.A., Hinde. J., Pogson, R., Wang, H., Marjo, C.E., Vasconcelos, P. & Michael Frese, M. (2022). A Lagerstätte from Australia provides insight into the nature of Miocene mesic ecosystems. *Science Advances* 8 eabm 1406, 07 Jan 2022: 11 pp.

Locality - Mc Graths Flat ~25 km northeast of Gulgong, NSW

Geocordinates   32.1° S; 149.7° E because the deposit is on private property only approximate coordinates are given to preserve confidentiality.

Palaeocoordinates   40.08° S; 149.8° E

Stratigraphic Information from McCurry et al (2022)
                         "similar to an oxbow lake".

Geological Age   early to middle Miocene

Age Mya   ~ 11 - 16

Meganisoptera [The order was formerly named Protodonata]

Repository   Australian Museum

Registration Number (s)   F.43142 and counterpart F.43141

Description

> Riek, E. F. (1968). Undescribed fossil insects from the Upper Permian of Belmont, New South Wales (with an appendix listing the described species). *Records of the Australian Museum* **27**(15): 303–310 [plate 45, fig.4].: 304

Etymology

> Gr. μέγας = great, large, mighty + Anisoptera (from Gr. ἄνισος = unequal + πτερόν = wing, because the hindwing is broader than the forewing).

Locality   Warner's Bay, Belmont, NSW

Geocordinates   33.0° S, 151.6° E

Palaeocoordinates   66.5° S, 144.3° E

Collector and Date   Presented O. Le M. Knight & D. Walker 1947

Lithological Information [from Knight (1950)]

> The rock in which the insect remains are found is a hard, very fine-grained chert about two feet six inches thick. Stratification is pronounced and well-defined joints cause the chert to break into rhomb-shaped blocks. The colour is light-grey to bluishgrey near its upper surface and becomes black towards the lower boundary.

Geological Age Late Permian: Lopingian Series, Changhsingian Stage (I.G. Percival in litt.)

Age Mya   254.0 - 252.3

Comments

> Meganisoptera is an extinct order of very large to gigantic insects, which may informally be called griffinflies. The order was formerly named Protodonata, the "proto-Odonata", for

their similar appearance and supposed relation to modern Odonata (damselflies and dragonflies).

Riek (1986) "These two impressions preserve the extreme apical portion of a very large wing that can be compared with species of Liadotypidae (order Meganisoptera)".

AM label gives Locality as Violettown nr. Warners Bay, NSW

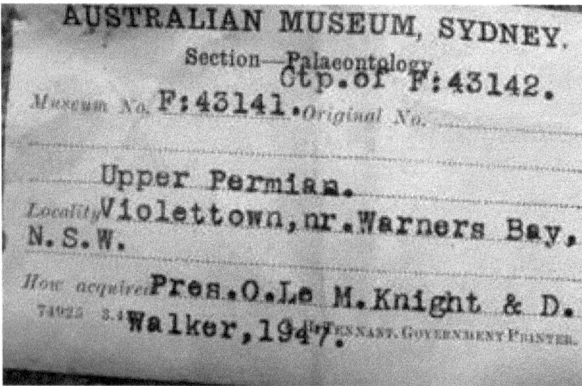

Figure 27 - Riek (1968) gives F. 43142 as the part and F. 43141 as the counterpart

Figure 28

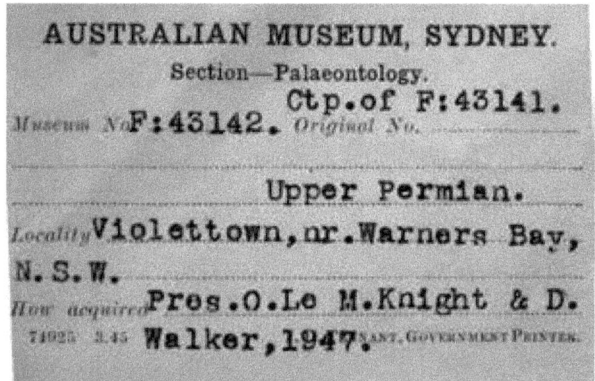

Mesophlebia antinodalis Tillyard, 1916

Holotype

Repository	QM	Natural History Museum
Registration Number(s)	GSQ 3a (holotype)	In 33279 counterpart (3b)

Specimen 3 is the type described in Tillyard (1916) while Specimen 127 is a paratype specimen to which Tillyard (1922) refers (as a 'heautotype').

Repository	Australian Museum	Natural History Museum
Registration Number(s)	Paratype: F.39270 (orig. no. 127a)	IN 33397 (counterpart)

Family Both Pritykina (1981) and Bechly (1997) synonymized Mesophlebiidae Tillyard, 1916 with Triassolestidae Tillyard, 1918

Original description

> Tillyard, R. J. (1916a). Descriptions of the fossil Insects; Mesozoic and Tertiary Insects of Queensland and New South Wales. Descriptions of the fossil Insects and stratigraphical features. *Queensland Geological Survey* (253) 11-7. [pp. 25-26; pl. 4, fig.2]

> Tillyard, R. J. (1922). Mesozoic Insects of Queensland. No. 9 Orthoptera, and additions to the Protorthoptera, Odonata, Hemiptera and Planipennia. *The Proceedings of the Linnean Society of New South Wales* 47:447-470. [pp. 456 – 458; pl. li, fig.31; text fig. 77] [p. 454; text fig. 76]

Etymology of genus name

> Gr. μέσος = middle + Gr. φλέψ (stem φλεβ–) = vein + adjectival suffix –ιος –ία –ιον = associated with, "middle vein" has no meaning so it is more likely that the morpheme meso- comes from Mesozoic (cf. Triassolestes, Triassophlebia)

Etymology of species name

In a section entitled THE PHYLOGENY OF THE NODUS IN THE DRAGON-FLY WING. Tillyard 1916:26-27) the author writes "The discovery of *Mesophlebia* gives us a very important clue to the phylogeny of that extraordinary and unique formation in the Dragon-fly wing known as the nodus." In the type description he enlarges on that with "The nodus of recent dragonflies differs from that in *Mesophlebia* in two important respects. Firstly, the joint is a much more complete one, the proximal and distal parts of the nodus being more closely fused. Secondly, the lower half of the nodal cross-vein has become bent at an obtuse angle to the rest ..."

Gr. prefix αντι- = instead of + L. *nodus* = knot (in Odonata, where the second main vein meets the leading edge of the wing) +L. suffix *–alis*= in connection with, relating to.

Locality - Ipswich Basin: Blackstone Formation: Denmark Hill Insect Bed, QLD

Geocordinates	27.6° S, 152.8° E
Palaeocoordinates	58.6° S, 101.0° E

Stratigraphic Information (from Paleobiology Database)

Interbedded sandstones and mudstones accumulated on levees bordering channels and graded laterally into floodplains where carbonaceous mudstones accumulated with thin crevasse splay sandstone beds.

The Insect bed is about 50 feet above the Bluff coal seam and 50 feet below the Aberdare coal seam. Fossil bed is 15 cm thick. Purdy & Cranfield (2013) reported an unpublished SHRIMP date of 226±2 Ma for the Brisbane Tuff. Therefore, the Blackstone Formation may be considered younger than 226 Ma in absolute age. Thus, the Ipswich Coal Measures above the Brisbane Tuff, which is to say, the succession from the Mount Crosby Formation to the top of the Blackstone Formation must now be considered Norian.

Geological Age	Late Triassic: Norian
Age Mya	221.5 - 205.6

Voucher Number from Original Description

"TYPE: Spec. 3a TYPE-COUNTERPART 3b (B.D. [Benjamin Dunstan] Coll.)" Tillyard (1922)

Other References   Fletcher (1971: 122).

Comments

Tierney et al. (2020) "There has been some confusion around whether the type specimens are the positive and negative imprints of the same individual. Contrary to the statement by Nel et al. (2002), specimen NHMUK In.33397 (not 'In.3397') is not the negative imprint of the holotype (NHMUK In.33279), but rather the negative imprint of the paratype, AM F39270. This is confirmed by the original numbering mentioned in Tillyard's accounts and still visible on the NHMUK specimens ('3b' on NHMUK In.33279, and '127b' on NHMUK In.33397; red paint), and based on the fact that both are negative imprints. The number '127a' is visible on the specimen AM F39270 (red paint). Incidentally, this explains discrepancies between the drawings provided by Nel et al. (2002), as they document distinct individuals."

Holotype

Figure 29-GSQ3a part

Figure 30 - n 33297 counterpart (GSQ 3b)

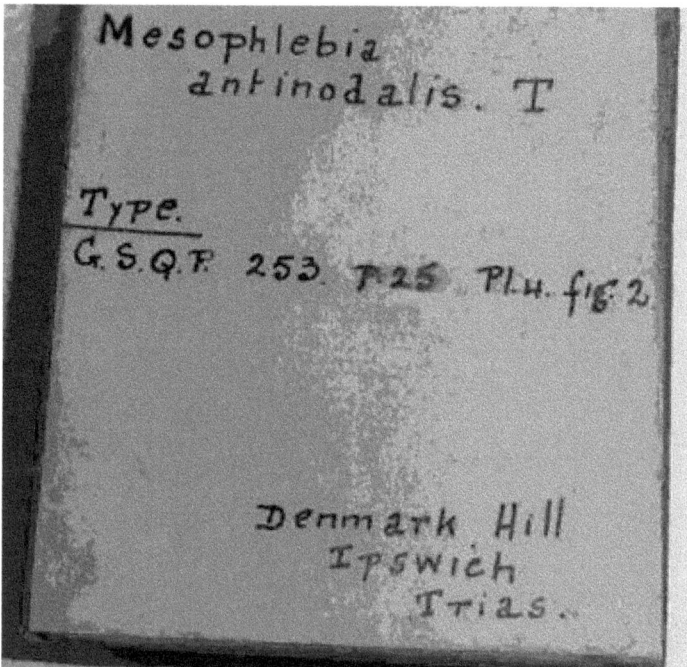

Figure 31 - GSQ 3a Dunstan storage box in QM & A. Rix (pers. comm.) [contra Tierney at al (2020:4) which says "current location of the positive imprint, '3a' in Tillyard 1916, unknown)"]

Paratype

Figure 32 - F.39270
part (GSQ 127a)

Figure 33 - In 33397
counterpart (GSQ 127b)

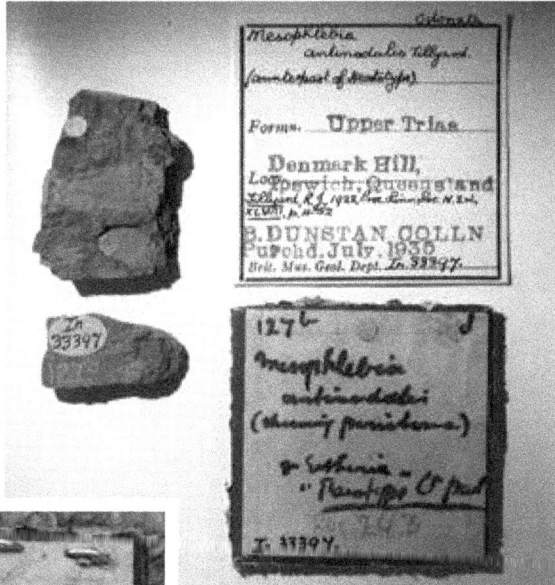

Figure 34 -
Dunstan Storage
Box for GSQ 127a

Mesophlebia antinodalis Tillyard, 1916

Repository   Queensland Museum

Registration Number(s)   QMF 58847

Description

Tierney et al 2020 "Herein the Australian species *Mesophlebia antinodalis* Tillyard, 1916 is redescribed on the basis of a new, subcomplete forewing."

Tierney et al. (2020) "The Australian specimen investigated herein is housed at the Queensland Museum (Geosciences Collection, Hendra). It bears the specimen number QMF 58847 (positive imprint; Fig. 1A, B). It was collected from a new locality provisionally numbered 'QLM 1307' near the town of Wondai, in the Burnett region of southeastern Queensland. The wing was preserved in a tuff together with plants (*Dicroidium* spp. and Calamitales) and spinicaudatans. As for its stratigraphic position, a minimum age constraint of 226.5 ± 1.6Ma was derived for the Aranbanga Volcanic Group based on U–Pb zircon dating of the intruding Mungore Granite (see Donchak et al. 2013 and references therein). Therefore, it is likely of Carnian, or possibly lowermost Norian, age.

Locality - QLM 1307 near Wondai (in the Burnett region of southeastern Queensland)

Geocordinates   26.3° S, 151.9° E

Palaeocoordinates   61.8° S, 129.5° E

Stratigraphic Information (from Tierney et al, (2020))

Preserved in tuff of the Arabanga Volcanic Group

Geological Age   Triassic: Carnian or possibly lowermost Norian

Age Ma   226.5 ± 1.6Ma

Mesophlebia tillyardi Handlirsch, 1939
(syn. *Mesophlebia antinodalis* Tillyard, 1916)

Repository	Australian Museum	NHMUK
Registration Number(s)	Paratype: F.39270 (orig. no. 127a)	IN33397 (counterpart)

Original description

> Handlirsch, A. (1939). Neue Untersuchungen über die fossilen Insekten mit Ergänzungen und Nachträgen sowie Ausblicken auf phylogenetische, palaeogeographische und allgemein biologische Probleme. II Teil. Annalen des Naturhistorischen Museums in Wien 49:1-240.

Etymology of species name

> An eponym honouring R.J. Tillyard

Comments

> Handlirsch (1939) "Was 1922 als *Mesophlebia antinodalis* beschrieben und abgebildet wird (fig. 75), erscheint mir hinlänglich verschieden, um mindestens eine eigene Species (wenn nicht ein Genus!) zu rechtfertigen: *Tillyardi* m. [What is described and depicted as *Mesophlebia antinodalis* in 1922 (fig. 75) seems to me to be sufficiently different to justify at least one species (if not a genus!): *tillyardi* m]".

> Cowley (1942) "Handlirsch (1939) considers that the two specimens described by Tillyard (1916, 1922) as *M. antinodalis* from the Trias of Australia belong to two species, and possibly to two genera, and has named the later specimen (of Tillyard, 1922) *M. tillyardi*. But it should be recollected that Tillyard (1922) suggested that the latter specimen might be a fore-wing, and the type-specimen of *M. antinodalis* a hind-wing, and further that as the type-specimen was not very well preserved in places, the differences between the specimens might not really be as great as they appear. Certainly if the apparent differences are real, Handlirsch's suggestion of a new genus and species

would seem to be justified, but until some attempt has been made to substantiate this by a re-examination of the type it seems to me best to relegate *M. tillyardi* to synonymy."

Nel & Paicheler (1994). "Handlirsch (1939: 11) crée l'espèce *Mesophlebia tillyardi* pour le spécimen 127a. Cowley (1942) met en synonymie *M. Tillyardi* avec *M. antinodalis*. [Handlirsch (1939: 11) created the species *Mesophlebia tillyardi* for the specimen 127a. Cowley (1942) puts *M. Tillyardi* in synonymy with *M. antinodalis*.]

Niwratia elongata Jell & Duncan 1986

Repository	Melbourne Museum	
Registration Number(s)	NMVP 102517 Siphonaptera	Jell & Duncan (1986) Fig 46E

Original description

Jell & Duncan (1986) Invertebrates, mainly insects, from the freshwater, Lower Cretaceous, Koonwarra Fossil Bed (Korumburra Group), South Gippsland, Victoria. *Memoirs of the Association of Australasian Palaeontologists* **3**:111-205. [pp. 166 - 168; figs. 42C, 46E]

Etymology of genus name

Jell & Duncan (1986:166) "The name of the nearby village of Tarwin, reversed" + feminine form of the Gr. suffix –ιος – ία –ιον = concerning.

Etymology of species name

Jell & Duncan (1986:167) "L. *elongatus,* – prolonged" in reference to "… legs extremely long and slender (each at least 2 mm from coxa to tip)"

Locality - Koonwarra Fossil Bed, VIC NMVPL425, Koonwarra

Geocordinates	38.6° S, 146.0° E
Palaeocoordinates	71.0° S, 121.6° E

Stratigraphic Information (from Paleobiology Database)

The Koonwarra Fossil Bed of South Gippsland, Australia, is ≈8 m thick, and the invertebrate fossils occur mainly on the lower strata just above an apatite layer dated 118 ± 5 million yr old and below a layer dated 115 ± 5 million yr old (Drinnan & Chambers 1986, Jell & Duncan 1986). Orig. assigned to Korumburra Group.

Numerous aquatic and semiaquatic insects in this bed, and the finely stratified mudstone that contains them, indicate a shallow pond with marshy edges that received periodic muddy influx from a larger adjacent lake.

Geological Age	Cretaceous: Late Aptian
Age MYA	122.46 to 112.6 Ma
Comments	

Jell & Duncan (1986:166) "The distinctive feature of this genus is the combination of long, slender legs with a typical siphonapteran body".

Riek (1970:746) discusses the occurrence of two fleas in the Koonawarra deposit. He postulates that at least one was associated with a furred animal, thereby "affect[ing] the zoography of the southern continents". They were not formally described until 1986 (Jell & Duncan).

Huang (2015: 507) examined the two species of fossil Siphonaptera from Koonwarra held in the Melbourne Museum and concluded "*Niwratia* … is in fact a libellulid larva of Odonata".

Zherikhin (2002: 366) agrees "(the illustrations in Jell & Duncan 1986, indicate that the unique type specimen is a probably young dragonfly nymph), "

Anderson (2018:32) concurs "This re-examination of the material confirms that the specimen is an anisopteran naiad, due to the presence of an anal pyramid and lack of a stylate proboscis."

Figure 35 -
Niwratia elongata
NMVP 102517

Peraphlebia tetrastichia Jell & Duncan, 1986

Repository   National Museum of Victoria

Registration Number(s)   NMVP 103204 A&B wing (was MUGD 3731 A&B) Jell & Duncan (1986) Fig 8D

Original description

> Jell, P. A. & Duncan, P. M. (1986). Invertebrates, mainly insects, from the freshwater, Lower Cretaceous, Koonwarra Fossil Bed (Korumburra Group), South Gippsland, Victoria. *Memoirs of the Association of Australasian Palaeontologists* **3**:111-205. [pp. 126-131; figs. 8-10]

Etymology of genus name

> Jell & Duncan (1986:126) "Greek, pera – beyond or very; and phlebos – vein"

> Gr. πέρᾰ = beyond+ Gr. πέρα (stem φλεβ–) = vein.

> Jell & Duncan (1986:129) "… it is considered to belong to the Mesophlebiidae because it retains the wide area between R3 and R4 with more than two rows of cells whereas other families of the Libelluloidea have the number of rows of cells in this area reduced to one or rarely as in some Libellulidae and Corduliidae to two." That means: more rows of cells = more veins as a distinguishing feature and a reference to the related *Mesophlebia* as well

Etymology of species name

> Jell & Duncan(1986:129) "Greek, tetra- four; and *stichia* – row or line" referring to "… there are four rows [of cells] at the wing margin in the fossil species."

> There is no Greek word stichia, but only στίχος = row, line + adjectival suffix –ios, –ía, –ion = associated with.

> Locality - PL425 Koonwarra Fossil Bed. Road cutting on South Gippsland Hwy, 1.5 miles W of Tarwin & 2.5 miles SE of Koonwarra (93.5 miles SE of Melbourne) (Parish of

Leongatha, 11.5 chains W of the NE corner of Allot. 87) (145 56 E)

Geocordinates	38.6° S, 145.56° E
Palaeocoordinates	77.0° S, 118.6° E
Collector and Date	collected by Talent, Duncan, Handby; 1961; 1962-1967

Stratigraphic Information (from Paleobiology Database)

The Koonwarra Fossil Bed of South Gippsland, Australia, is ≈8 m thick, and the invertebrate fossils occur mainly on the lower strata just above an apatite layer dated 118 ± 5 million yr old and below a layer dated 115 ± 5 million yr old (Drinnan & Chambers 1986, Jell & Duncan 1986). Orig. assigned to Korumburra Group.

Numerous aquatic and semiaquatic insects in this bed, and the finely stratified mudstone that contains them, indicate a shallow pond with marshy edges that received periodic muddy influx from a larger adjacent lake.

Geological Age	Cretaceous: Late Aptian
Age MYA	122.46 to 112.6 Ma

Type specimen, a wing (Apical fragment).

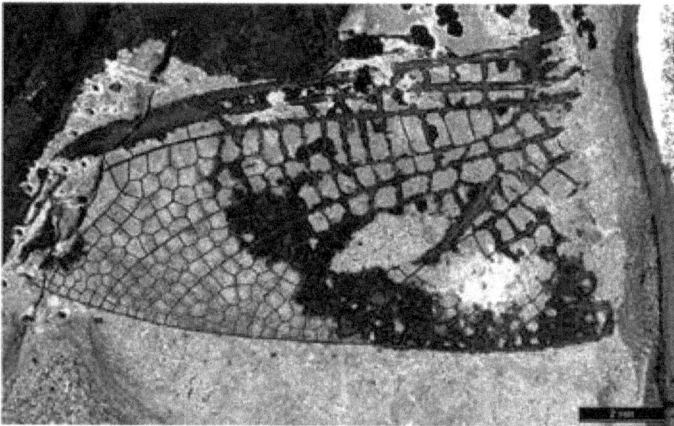

Figure 36 NMVP 103204A

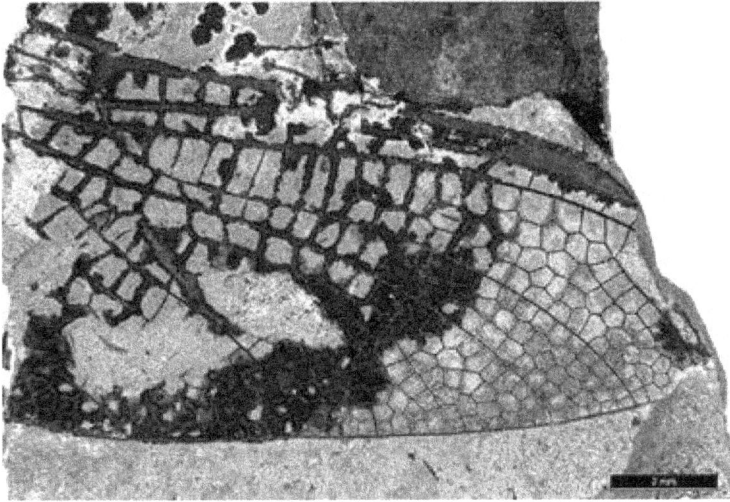

Figure 37 - NMVP 103204B

Peraphlebia tetrastichia Jell & Duncan, 1986 (larvae)

Repository	National Museum of Victoria
Registration Number(s)	[Figure numbers from Jell & Duncan (1986)]

NMVP 103212 immature larva   Fig 8A

NMV P123050 A&B (Formerly MUGD 3731 A&B) mature larva   Fig 8B,C

NMVP 102518A mature larva   Fig 10

Original description

Jell, P. A. & Duncan, P. M. (1986). Invertebrates, mainly insects, from the freshwater, Lower Cretaceous, Koonwarra Fossil Bed (Korumburra Group), South Gippsland, Victoria. *Memoirs of the Association of Australasian Palaeontologists* **3**:111-205. [pp. 126-131; figs. 8-10]

Locality - Koonwarra Fossil Bed, VIC

Geocordinates	38.6° S, 146.0° E
Palaeocoordinates	77.0° S, 118.6° E

Stratigraphic Information (from Paleobiology Database)

The Koonwarra Fossil Bed of South Gippsland, Australia, is ≈8 m thick, and the invertebrate fossils occur mainly on the lower strata just above an apatite layer dated 118 ± 5 million yr old and below a layer dated 115 ± 5 million yr old (Drinnan & Chambers 1986, Jell & Duncan 1986). Orig. assigned to Korumburra Group.

Numerous aquatic and semiaquatic insects in this bed, and the finely stratified mudstone that contains them, indicate a shallow pond with marshy edges that received periodic muddy influx from a larger adjacent lake.

Geological Age	Cretaceous: Late Aptian
Age MYA	122.46 to 112.6 Ma

Comments

Identification by association with adult – Jell & Duncan (1986) "Although some doubt exists as to whether the three specimens listed above or any two of them are conspecific they are here considered as such because no other anisopteran has been found in this very large collection and also there is no reason why they could not represent three stages in development of the one species. Despite rather negative evidence, we consider this association of convenience a reasonable step until better material becomes available."

Nel & Paicheler (1994: 331) cast doubt on this association of larva and adult "JELL & DUNCAN n'ont aucune preuve que ces larves soient celles de Peraphlebia tetrastichia (à moins qu'ils n'aient réussi l'élevage des larves de Libellules fossiles) et ne peuvent fonder leur raisonnement sur cette hypothèse indémontrable.[JELL & DUNCAN have no proof that these larvae are those of *Peraphlebia* tetrastichia (unless they have succeeded in breeding fossil dragonfly larvae) and cannot base their reasoning on this unprovable hypothesis.]

Anderson (2018: 33), quoting Fleck et al. (2002), also argues that it is not legitimate to link a larva with an adult unless it has been raised under laboratory conditions and the transformation observed, thus rendering the association inconclusive.

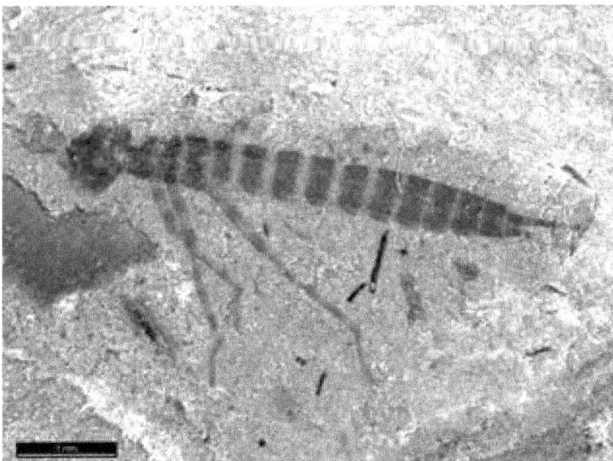

Figure 38 - NMVP 103212 Immature larva according to Jell & Duncan (1986)

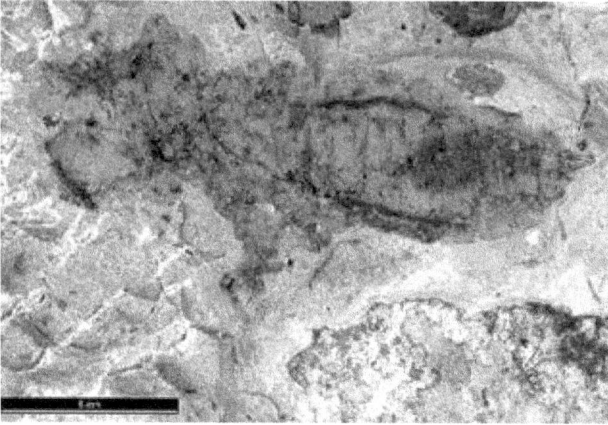

Figure 39 - NMVP
102518 A

Figure 40 -
NMVP 123050 A
(previously MUGB
3731A) part

Figure 41 - NMVP
123050 B (previously
MUGB 3731B)
counterpart (Note –
orientation of photo is
different from that of part)

Perissophlebia multiseriata Tillyard, 1918

Repository	Queensland Museum	Natural History Museum
Registration Number(s)	Holotype; Specimen No. 203 a, (part). (Coll. Queensland Geological Survey) GSQ3a	In 33467 (= GSQ3b) (counterpart)

Original description

> Tillyard, R. J. (1918). Mesozoic Insects of Queensland. No. 3 Odonata and Protodonata. *The Proceedings of the Linnean Society of New South Wales* **43**: 417-436.[pp.424 – 425, text fig. 13]

Etymology of genus name

Gr. περισσός = beyond the regular number or size + Gr. φλέψ (stem φλεβ–) = vein

Etymology of species name

> Tillyard (1918: 423) "Hence we see that ... *Perissophlebia* stands as the most densely veined of all known Odonata."

> L. *multus, -a,-um* = many + L.series = row + *-atus –ata –atum* = marked with, equipped with

> Both the genus and species names refer to the same character.

Locality - "Ipswich Fossil Bed" Denmark Hill Fossil Bed, QLD

Geocordinates	27.6° S, 152.8° E
Palaeocoordinates	58.6° S, 101.0° E

Stratigraphic Information (from Paleobiology Database)

> Interbedded sandstones and mudstones accumulated on levees bordering channels and graded laterally into floodplains where carbonaceous mudstones accumulated with thin crevasse splay sandstone beds.

The Insect bed is about 50 feet above the Bluff coal seam and 50 feet below the Aberdare coal seam. Fossil bed is 15 cm thick. Purdy & Cranfield (2013) reported an unpublished SHRIMP date of 226±2 Ma for the Brisbane Tuff. Therefore, the Blackstone Formation may be considered younger than 226 Ma in absolute age. Thus, the Ipswich Coal Measures above the Brisbane Tuff, which is to say, the succession from the Mount Crosby Formation to the top of the Blackstone Formation must now be considered Norian.

Geological Age	Late Triassic: Norian
Age MYA	221.5 - 205.6 Ma

Voucher Number from Original Description

Tillyard (1918) "Type, Specimen No. 203 a b (part and counterpart). (Coll. Queensland Geological Survey)."

Figure 42 - GSQ 203a

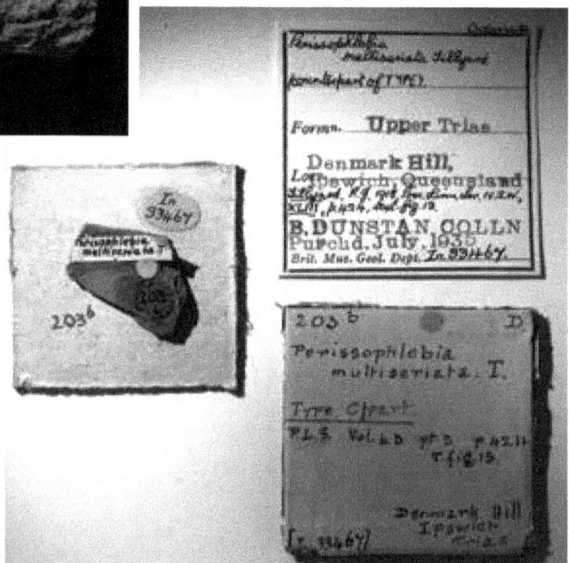

Figure 43 - In 33467

Polytaxineura stanleyi Tillyard, 1935

Family - Polytaxineuridae although Jell 2004 places it in the Permaeschnidae. Carpenter (1992) considers Permaeschniidae to be a subjective synonym. Tillyard (1935a:375) "This family... also includes ... the imperfectly preserved genus *Permaeschna* ... Should it, however, prove later on to belong to the same family as *Polytaxineura* then the name of the family must be changed to Permaeschnidae Martynov, since Martynov actually defined this family in 1931."

Repository	Natural History Museum
Registration Number(s)	In 46395;
	In 45781 part and counterpart (No ID on label but same locality as In 46395)
	In 45360; (no ID on label but same locality as In 46395)

Original description

> Tillyard, R. J. (1935a). Upper Permian insects of New South Wales. Part 4. The order Odonata. *Proceedings of the Linnean Society of New South Wales* 60: 374-384. [pp. 376-379; pl. xii, figs 1 – 3; text figs. 1 – 3]

Etymology of genus name

> Tillyard (1935a:375-6) states "The spaces between Mspl, the basal portion of 1A, Aspl and the posterior border are all filled with a polygonal network of cellules for the most part regularly arranged; this formation has suggested the name of the genus." Gr. πολύς = many + τάξις = arrangement + νεῦρος = nerve, or wing veins in entomology.

> -neura (in odonate names) = veined; the philological explanation is somewhat complicated: the element in question is the adjectival Greek morpheme –neuros = veined; but its feminine ending in Greek is –os but for nomenclature it is transferred to Latin, where the feminine form becomes –a

Endersby

Etymology of species name

> Tillyard (1935a:374) "The first discovery of a fragment of a dragonfly wing was made by Mr. T.H. Pincombe in 1931, in a piece of rock from Warner's Bay. It is a small piece of a rather large wing, showing the nodus and portions of the costa, subcosta, radius and radial sector around it, as far as the beginning of the pterostigma. A further discovery of portion of the posterior margin and cellules just above it, of a much crumpled Odonate wing, was also made by Mr. Pincombe in 1931.

> "The above-mentioned material was considered by me to be too fragmentary for description by itself. The search for a more complete wing has now at last been rewarded, twenty years or so after the original discovery of the Belmont Beds by Mr. John Mitchell. by the finding of a nearly complete forewing by Mr. M.S. Stanley on 2nd April of this year, in a piece of grey shale brought by him from Warner's Bay. Mr. Stanley is to be heartily congratulated on this fine discovery, which is commemorated in the naming of the species in his honour in this paper. The other fragmentary remains are also dealt with in this paper."

Locality	Warner's Bay, Belmont, NSW
Geocordinates	33.0° S, 151.6° E
Palaeocoordinates	66.5° S, 144.3° E
Collector and Date	

see Etymology of Species

Locality	Warner's Bay, Belmont, NSW
Geocordinates	33.0° S, 151.6° E
Palaeocoordinates	66.5° S, 144.3° E
Lithological Information (from Knight (1950))	

> The rock in which the insect remains are found is a hard, very fine-grained chert about two feet six inches thick. Stratification is pronounced and well-defined joints cause the chert to break into rhomb-shaped blocks. The colour is light-grey to bluishgrey near its upper surface and becomes black towards the lower boundary.

Geological Age   Late Permian: Changhsingian

Age MYA   254.0 - 252.3 Ma

Voucher Number from Original Description

> Tillyard (1935a) "Holotype, Specimen S 343, A, B and C: A, obverse impression of forewing and small portion of hindwing, with apex to left; B, basal half of the reverse impression of same; C, anterior portion of distal half of reverse impression same."

Comments

> Numbered S343 A, B and C in Tillyard (1935) but repository not stated.

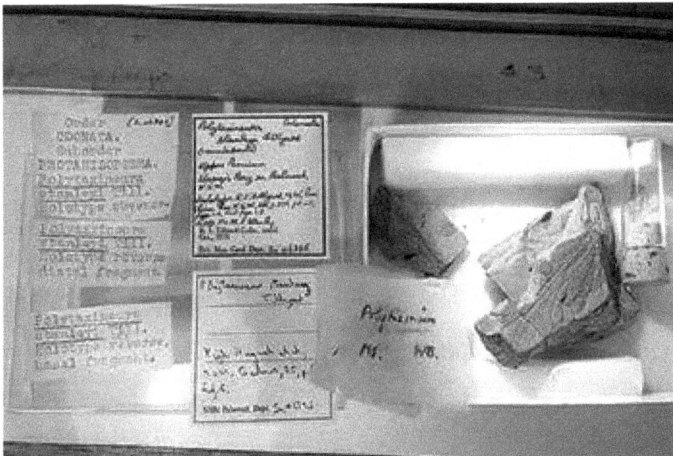

Figure 44
- In 46395
NHMUK

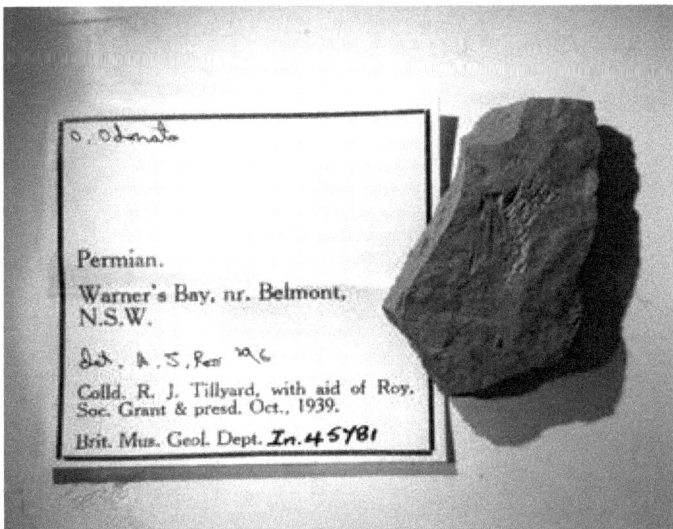

Figure 45
- In 45781
NHMUK

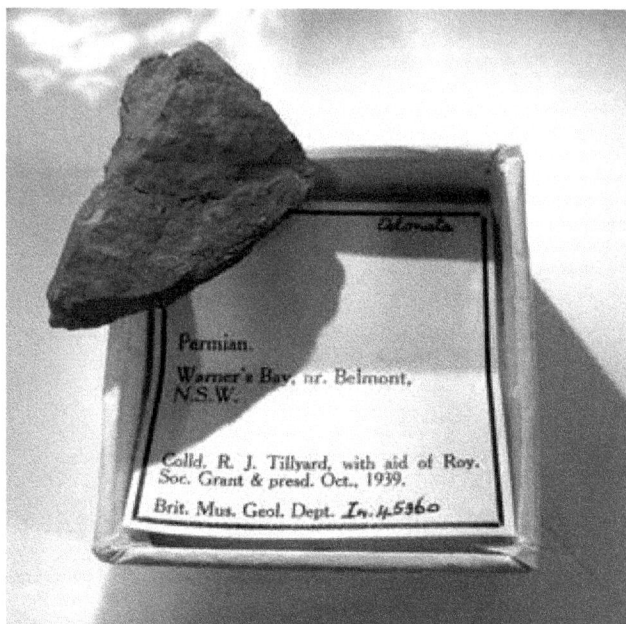

Figure 46 - In 45360 NHMUK

Samarura Brauer et al., 1889

Repository	Queensland Museum
Registration Number(s	QMF 12996 a,b part and counterpart (Jell 2004)

Original description of genus

> Brauer, F., Redtenbacher, J. & Ganglbauer, L. (1889). Fossile Insekten aus der Juraformation Ost-Sibiriens. *Mémoires de l'Académie Impériale des Sciences de St.-Pétersbourg, VII Série* 36(15):1-22. [pp. 7 – 9; figs. 6 – 10

Description of this specimen

> Rozefelds, A. C. (1985). A Fossil Zygopteran Nymph (Insecta: Odonata) from the Late Triassic Aberdare Conglomerate: Southeast Queensland. *Proceedings of the Royal Society of Queensland* **96**:25-32

Etymology of genus name

> L. *samera (samara)* = the seed of the elm (Samara - a dry indehiscent usually one-seeded winged fruit [as of an ash or elm tree]) + Gr οὐρά = tail, alluding to the larval anal appendages.

Locality - Ipswich Basin: Aberdare Conglomerate: Bundamba Group: Brassall Quarry, QLD

Geocordinates	27.5° S, 152.4° E
Palaeocoordinates	59.3° S, 140.5° E
Collector and Date	

Eileen Mack

Stratigraphic Information [From A field guide to "Sediments and fossils of the Ipswich Basin. Edited by W. F. Willmott (1986) An excursion organized by the Geological Society of Australia (Queensland Division)].

The overlying Brassall sub-Group, comprising the Tivoli and Blackstone Formations, contains fluvial sandstones, mudstones, and coal seams.

Geological Age   Late Triassic: Rhaetian
Age Mya   205.6 to 125.45 Ma
Voucher Number from Original Description

Rozefelds (1985) "QMF1299Ga,b from the Brassall Quarry, Ipswich, Queensland."

Comments

Zygoptera larva

Figure 47 - QMF 12996a part

Figure 48 - QMF 12996b counterpart

Tillyardomyrmeleon petermilleri Henrotay *et al.*, 1997

Repository	Natural History Museum
Registration Number(s)	Holotype In 46119

Original description

> Henrotay, M., Nel, A., Jarzembowski, E. A. (1997). New protomyrmeleontid damselflies from the Triassic of Australia and the Liassic of Luxembourg, with the description of *Tillyardomyrmeleon petermilleri* gen. nov. and spec. nov. Archizygoptera: Protomyrmeleontidae. *Odonatologica* 26(4): 395-404. [pp. 396 - 397; fig. 1]

Etymology of genus name

> Henrotay et al (1997) "After Tillyard and *Myrmeleon*"; [***Myrmeleon*** is an ant-lion genus]

Etymology of species name

> Henrotay et al (1997) "After the late Dr Peter Miller, Odonata specialist".

> In 1962 Miller left Uganda to become Lecturer in Zoology at Oxford University, where from 1964 until his retirement in 1994 he was Fellow and Tutor at the Queen's College. From the early 1980s Miller focused his research on dragonflies, a group of insects for which he had developed a strong affection while in Uganda. His highly developed skills - for interpreting subtle elements of behaviour, for micro-anatomical dissection and for quantifying neural processes - allowed him to reveal much of the structural and behavioural framework on which dragonfly reproduction is based. [*The Independent* Sunday 05 May 1996]

Locality - Sydney Basin: Hawkesbury Sandstone: Beacon Hill, Brookvale, near Manly, NSW. Presumably former Beacon Hill shale quarry. "the brick-pits of the Manly Rick and Tile Coy., Beacon Hill, Brookvale, which is near the coast, about three miles north of Port Jackson, New South Wales." Wade (1935)

Geocordinates	33.75° S; 151.26° E
Palaeocoordinates	68.0° S; 137.3° E

Stratigraphic Information [from Paleobiology Database, in turn, based on Jell (2004)]

> "This mudstone lens may be interpreted as a lacustrine interval on a quartz sandstone coastal plain and from the fauna a freshwater environment is most probable."

Geological Age	(Middle) Triassic: Anisian
Age MYA	circa 240-238 Ma

Voucher Number from Original Description

"Holotype: Specimen In 46119, Tillyard coll., Natural History Museum, Palaeontology Department, London. UK."

Other References

Whitehouse (2016)

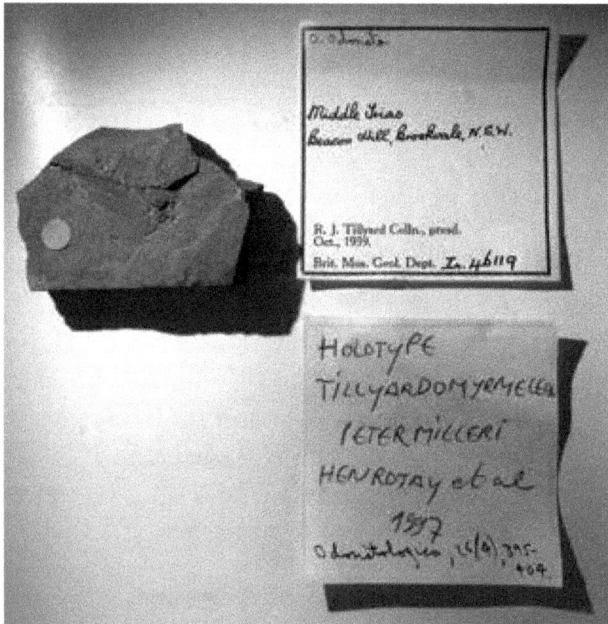

Figure 49 - In 46119 Holotype

Triassagrion australiense Tillyard, 1922

Family Protomyrmelontidae [***Myrmeleon*** is an ant-lion genus in the subfamily Myrmeleontinae]

Repository	Australian Museum	Natural History Museum
Registration Number(s)	Holotype F. 39253 (orig. no. 290a) Originally GSQ290	In 33544 (= BD290b) In 32925 part and counterpart. This specimen has no species name on the NHMUK label so be aware of the caveats expressed in the Comments section of the entry for Not Determined (Denmark Hill). In 32972 In 33126 counterpart (S453) In 33226 counterpart (S58b)

Original description

Tillyard, R. J. (1922). Mesozoic Insects of Queensland. No. 9 Orthoptera, and additions to the Protorthoptera, Odonata, Hemiptera and Planipennia. *The Proceedings of the Linnean Society of New South Wales* **47**:447-470. [pp. 456 – 458; pl. li, fig.31; text fig. 77]

Etymology of genus name

Triassic Gr τριάς = group of three (because it is divisible (in Germany) into three rock formations (Buntsandstein, Muschelkalk, Keuper) + -ic, English suffix = having characteristics of (derived from L. –*icus*, –*ica*, –*icum* (= belonging to) + *Agrion* (the name established by Fabricius in1775 to contain all of the Zygoptera. It is derived from Gr. ἄγριος = wild)

Etymology of species name

Australia, derived from L. *auster* (stem *austro–*) = south wind, hence south + L. suffix *–ensis* = belonging to.

Locality - Ipswich Basin: Blackstone Formation: Denmark Hill Insect Bed, QLD

Geocordinates	27.6° S, 152.8° E
Palaeocoordinates	58.6° S, 101.0° E

Stratigraphic Information (from Paleobiology Database)

Interbedded sandstones and mudstones accumulated on levees bordering channels and graded laterally into floodplains where carbonaceous mudstones accumulated with thin crevasse splay sandstone beds.

The Insect bed is about 50 feet above the Bluff coal seam and 50 feet below the Aberdare coal seam. Fossil bed is 15 cm thick. Purdy & Cranfield (2013) reported an unpublished SHRIMP date of 226±2 Ma for the Brisbane Tuff. Therefore, the Blackstone Formation may be considered younger than 226 Ma in absolute age. Thus, the Ipswich Coal Measures above the Brisbane Tuff, which is to say, the succession from the Mount Crosby Formation to the top of the Blackstone Formation must now be considered Norian.

Geological Age	Late Triassic: Norian
Age MYA	221.5 - 205.6 Ma

Voucher Number from Original Description

"Type, Specimen 290a (reverse), in Coll. Queensland Geol. Survey, Brisbane."

Other References   Fletcher (1971). [p. 130]

Comments

Nel et al (2005) "Although very complete, there are some small errors in the original description and drawing of Tillyard (1922). We had the opportunity to examine the counterpart of the holotype, which is stored at the British Museum of Natural History (specimen In 33544). We amend the original description as follows: only two rows of cells between RA and IR1, opposite pterostigma; RP3/4 not distally divided into two branches; four rows of cells between IR2 and RP2 along posterior wing margin; AA and AP are completely fused."

Although the AM label gives the part number of the holotype as 290, Parfrey's (2005) catalogue does not hold a record of this number, nor for this species.

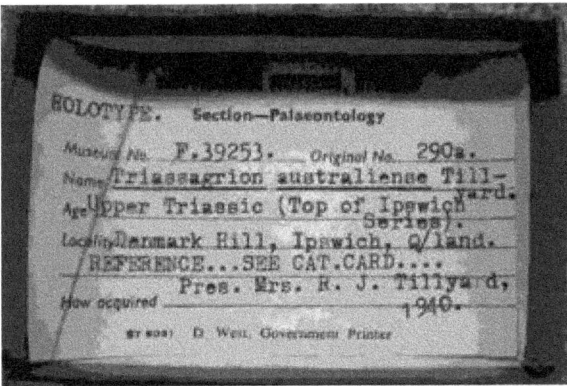

Figure 50 - F. 39353

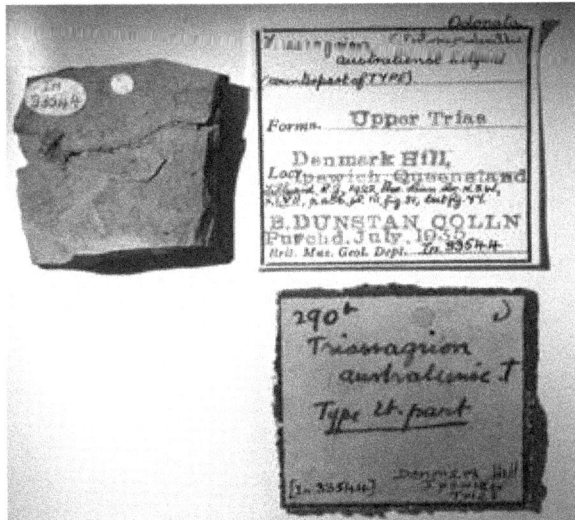

Figure 51- In 33544 counterpart

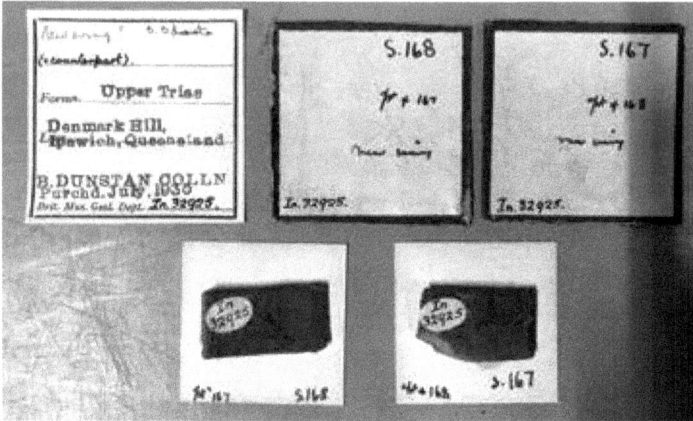

Figure 52 - In 32925 part and counterpart

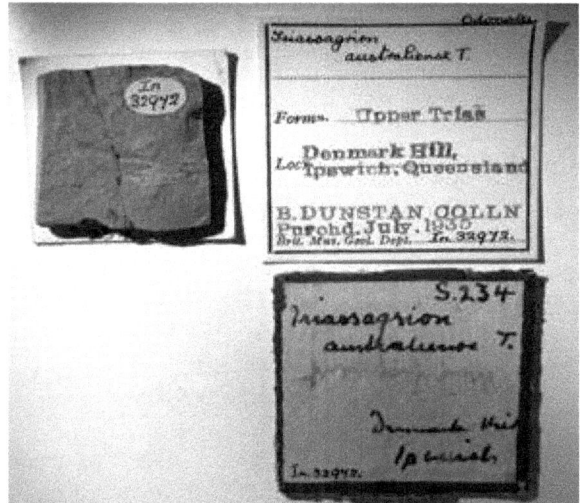

Figure 53 - In 32972

Figure 54 - In 33126

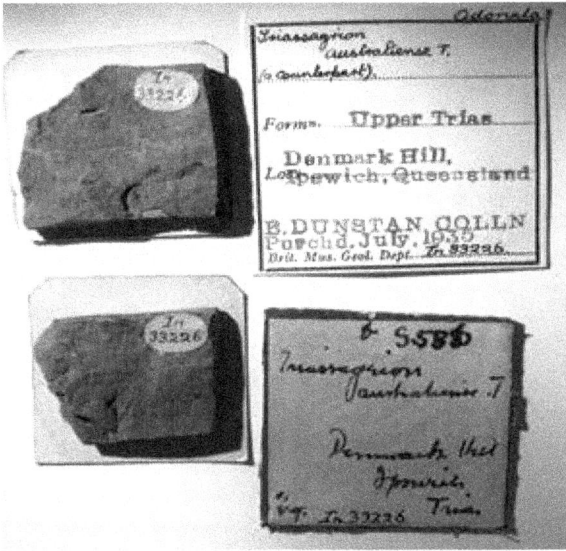

Figure 55 - In 33226

Triassolestes epiophlebioides Tillyard, 1918

Repository	Australian Museum	Natural History Museum
Registration Number(s)	Holotype: F. 39266 (orig. GSQ 205a)	In 33469 counterpart of type

Original description

> Tillyard, R. J. (1918). Mesozoic Insects of Queensland. No. 3 Odonata and Protodonata. *The Proceedings of the Linnean Society of New South Wales* **43**:417-436 [pp. 419-422; text figs. 11, 12b]

Etymology of genus name

> Triassic Gr τριάς = group of three (because it is divisible (in Germany) into three rock formations (Buntsandstein, Muschelkalk, Keuper) + -ic, English suffix = having characteristics of (derived from L. *–icus, –ica, –icum* (= belonging to) + genus name *Lestes* (Gr. ληστής = a robber or pirate)

Etymology of species name

> Tillyard (1918:121) "A close resemblance to *Epiophlebia* is shown in the levels of the origins of the branches of M, and in the shape and venation of the discoidal field and the two longitudinal areas of the wing lying below it."

> In a footnote to a review of Needham, J. G. (1903) A genealogic study of dragon-fly wing venation. *Proceedings United States National Museum* 26: 703-764, Calvert (1903:208) renamed the genus *Palaeophlebia* Selys 1889 (which was preoccupied by *Palaeophlebia* Brauer 1889) as *Epiophlebia* and gave its derivation thus "from ἐπιὼν [≈ coming upon ..., additional; present participle of ἔπειμι] and φλεψ, φλερος (sic)".

Locality - Ipswich Basin: Blackstone Formation: Denmark Hill Insect Bed, QLD

Geocordinates	27.6° S, 152.8° E
Palaeocoordinates	58.6° S, 101.0° E

Stratigraphic Information (from Paleobiology Database)

Interbedded sandstones and mudstones accumulated on levees bordering channels and graded laterally into floodplains where carbonaceous mudstones accumulated with thin crevasse splay sandstone beds.

The Insect bed is about 50 feet above the Bluff coal seam and 50 feet below the Aberdare coal seam. Fossil bed is 15 cm thick. Purdy & Cranfield (2013) reported an unpublished SHRIMP date of 226±2 Ma for the Brisbane Tuff. Therefore, the Blackstone Formation may be considered younger than 226 Ma in absolute age. Thus, the Ipswich Coal Measures above the Brisbane Tuff, which is to say, the succession from the Mount Crosby Formation to the top of the Blackstone Formation must now be considered Norian.

Geological Age   Late Triassic: Norian

Age MYA   221.5 - 205.6 Ma

Voucher Number from Original Description

"Type, Specimen No. 205a, (Coll. Queensland Geological Survey)."

Other References   Fletcher (1971). [p. 130]

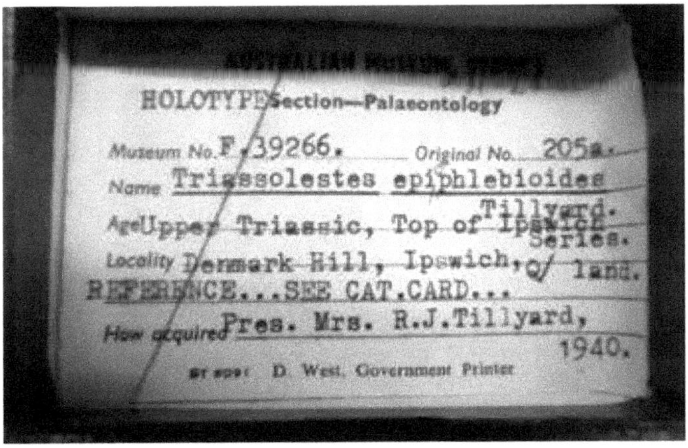

Figure 56 - F 39266

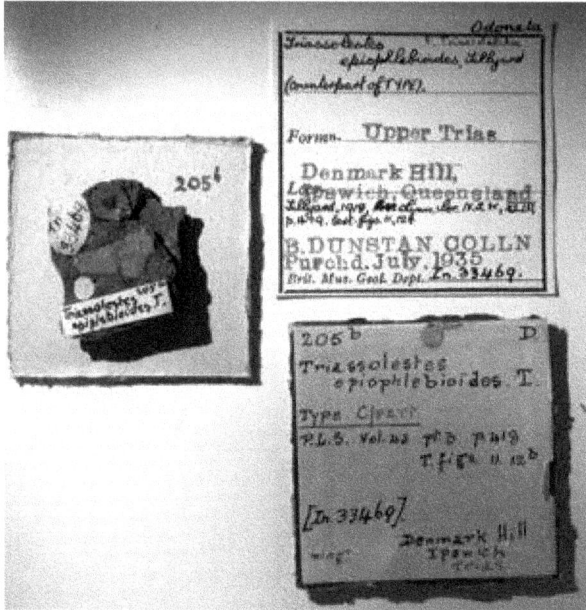

Figure 57 - In33469 counterpart

Triassophlebia stigmatica Tillyard, 1922

Repository	Australian Museum	Natural History Musem
Registration Number(s)	Holotype F. 39267 (Originally GSQI82)	In 33352 (= BD82b)

Original description

> Tillyard, R. J. (1922). Mesozoic Insects of Queensland. No. 9 Orthoptera, and additions to the Protorthoptera, Odonata, Hemiptera and Planipennia. *The Proceedings of the Linnean Society of New South Wales* **47**:447-470. [p. 454; text fig. 76]

Etymology of genus name

> Triassic Gr τριάς = group of three (because it is divisible (in Germany) into three rock formations (Buntsandstein, Muschelkalk, Keuper) + -ic, English suffix = having characteristics of (derived from L. *–icus, –ica, –icum* (= belonging to) plus Gr. φλέψ (stem φλεβ–) = vein + adjectival suffix –ιος –α –ον = associated with.

Etymology of species name

> While Tillyard does not explain his choice of epithet there are two passages of relevance in the species description" "R somewhat thickened below pterostigma, but not so strongly as in *Mesophlebia antinodalis.*" and "M2 arising from M as a strongly diverging vein which almost at once approaches Ms very closely, being separated from it only by a single row of very narrow cellules; further distad, below the level of the pterostigma …". However in the description of the new genus *Triassophlebia* he writes "*Pterostigma* elongated, about twice as long as in *Mesophlebia.*"

> Latinised from Gr. στίγμα = a prick, puncture, mark (in dragonfly names often used for the pterostigma) + suffix –(τ)ικός –ή –όν = pertaining to

Locality - Ipswich Basin: Blackstone Formation: Denmark Hill Insect Bed, QLD

Geocordinates	27.6° S, 152.8° E
Palaeocoordinates	58.6° S, 101.0° E

Stratigraphic Information (from Paleobiology Database)

Interbedded sandstones and mudstones accumulated on levees bordering channels and graded laterally into floodplains where carbonaceous mudstones accumulated with thin crevasse splay sandstone beds.

The Insect bed is about 50 feet above the Bluff coal seam and 50 feet below the Aberdare coal seam. Fossil bed is 15 cm thick. Purdy & Cranfield (2013) reported an unpublished SHRIMP date of 226±2 Ma for the Brisbane Tuff. Therefore, the Blackstone Formation may be considered younger than 226 Ma in absolute age. Thus, the Ipswich Coal Measures above the Brisbane Tuff, which is to say, the succession from the Mount Crosby Formation to the top of the Blackstone Formation must now be considered Norian.

Geological Age	Late Triassic: Norian
Age MYA	221.5 - 205.6 Ma

Voucher Number from Original Description

"Type, Specimen No. 82a in Coll. Queensland Geological Survey, Brisbane."

Other References   Fletcher (1971). [p. 130]

Comments

Odonatoptera *incertae sedis* according to Nel et al. 2002 [pp. 191-192]

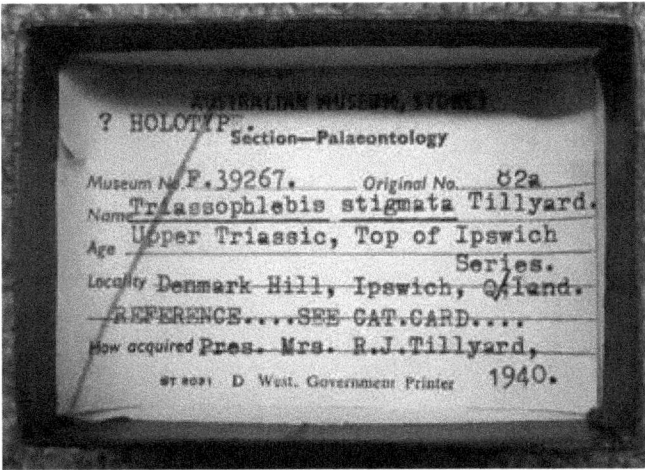

Figure 58 - F.39267
label

Figure 59 - F. 39267
part

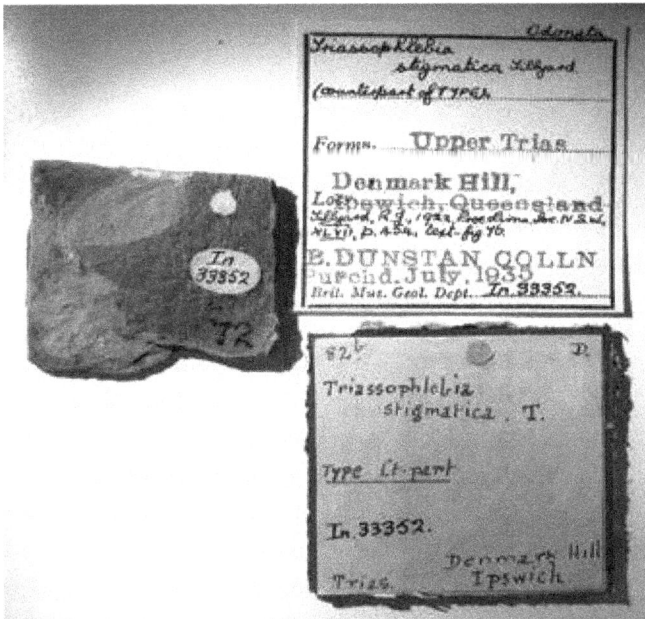

Figure 60 - In33352
counterpart

Not Determined (AM Display Specimen)

Repository   Australian Museum
Registration Number(s)   F. 39175
Comments

    Australian Museum records show that the specimen as having been donated by "Mr. R. J. Tillyard 1938". However as that is in the year after his death it is more likely that it was donated by his wife but recorded under his name.

Not determined (Beacon Hill)

Repository   Natural History Museum

Registration Number(s)   In 46112; In 46116 part and counterpart

(No species name on either NHMUK label.) A.J. Ross considered them to be possibly Odonata.

Stratigraphic Information [from Paleobiology Database, in turn, based on Jell (2004)]

> "This mudstone lens may be interpreted as a lacustrine interval on a quartz sandstone coastal plain and from the fauna a freshwater environment is most probable."

Geological Age   (Middle) Triassic: Anisian

Age MYA   circa 240-238 Ma

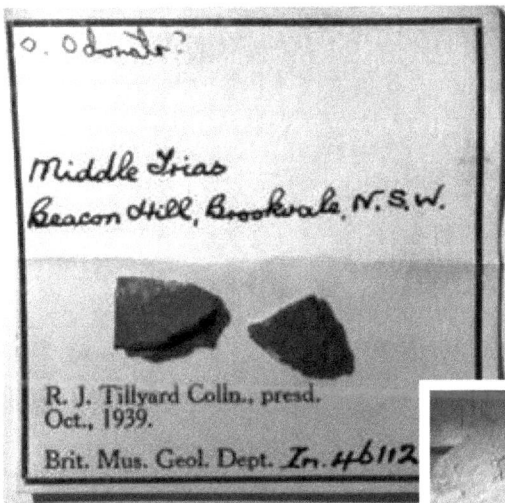

Figure 61 - In 46112 part and counterpart

Figure 62 - In 46116 part and counterpart

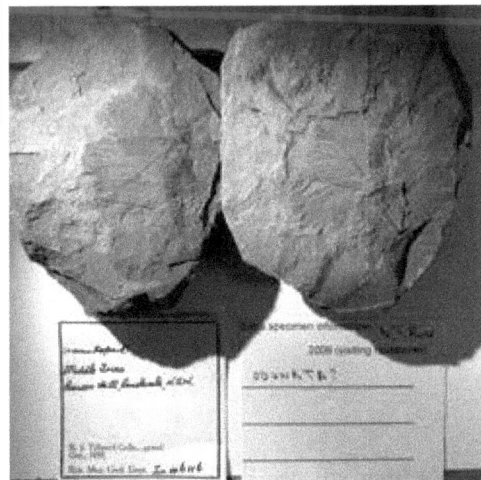

Not Determined (Denmark Hill)

Part and counterpart (No ID on label)

Repository   Natural History Museum (London)

Registration Number(s)   In 33519

Original description (possibly)

> Tillyard, R. J. (1919) Mesozoic Insects of Queensland No. 6. Blattoidea. *Proceedings of the Linnean Society of New South Wales* 44: 358—382.

Locality - Ipswich Basin: Blackstone Formation: Denmark Hill Insect Bed, QLD

Geocordinates   27.6° S, 152.8° E

Palaeocoordinates   58.6° S, 101.0° E

Stratigraphic Information (from Paleobiology Database)

> Interbedded sandstones and mudstones accumulated on levees bordering channels and graded laterally into floodplains where carbonaceous mudstones accumulated with thin crevasse splay sandstone beds.

> The Insect bed is about 50 feet above the Bluff coal seam and 50 feet below the Aberdare coal seam. Fossil bed is 15 cm thick. Purdy & Cranfield (2013) reported an unpublished SHRIMP date of 226±2 Ma for the Brisbane Tuff. Therefore, the Blackstone Formation may be considered younger than 226 Ma in absolute age. Thus, the Ipswich Coal Measures above the Brisbane Tuff, which is to say, the succession from the Mount Crosby Formation to the top of the Blackstone Formation must now be considered Norian.

Geological Age   Late Triassic: Norian

Age MYA   221.5 - 205.6 Ma

Other References   Fletcher (1971). [p. 130]

Comments

Nel et.al (2005) attribute this specimen to *Triassolestes australiense*.

The number "262:" appears on the storage box of this fossil, apparently in Dunstan's handwriting, and it was the counterpart of the holotype sold to the British Museum (Natural History) as part of the Dunstan Collection.

Parfrey, S.M. (1996) gives the following information about that fossil:

262 *Samaroblatta intercalata* Tillyard HOLOTYPE

Locality: Denmark Hill, Ipswich.

Formation: Blackstone Fm.

Age: Triassic

Collector: B. Dunstan

The specimen was deemed to be Odonata by the London Museum. L. Stevens (in litt.) "I expect it was a previous curator, Andrew Ross. He sorted out the entire collection when it came over to the palaeo collections many years ago. As a higher group, it is likely to be a preliminary identification to aid management of collections and not to be taken as an expert ID. It might be that the person who made the label did not get round to checking the Survey's catalogue."

As this seems to be an implausible explanation, and giving credence to the opinion of Nel et.al (2005), it will be retained as an Odonate in this catalogue.

These observations also put in doubt the identification of In 32925, In 45360, In 45781, In 46112 and In 46116 which have similar handwritten labels with no species' determination. In 45781, from Warner's Bay, has a note that the determination as O. Odonata was made by A.J. Ross while In 46112, from Beacon Hill, has doubts about the order giving "Odonata ?"

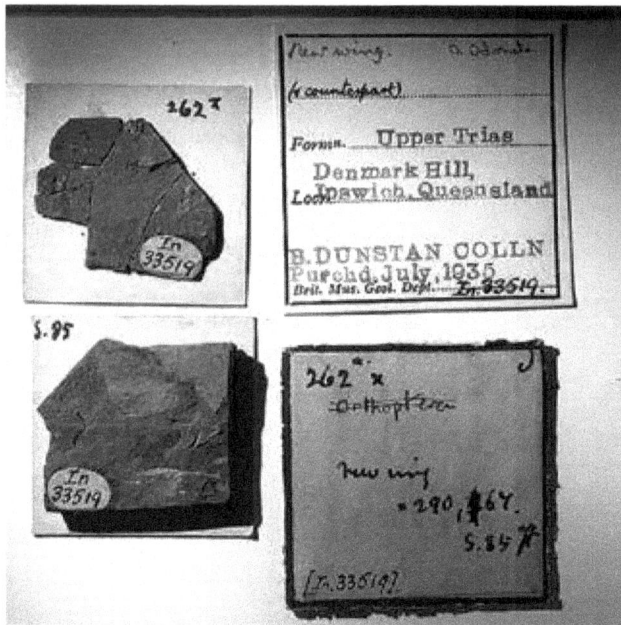

Figure 63 - In 33519

Not Determined (Dinmore)

Reference

Riek, E. F. (1952). Fossil insects from the Tertiary sediments at Dinmore, Queensland. University of Queensland Papers, Department of Geology 4: 17-22, pl. 1.

Locality - Dinmore clay pits, QLD

Geocordinates   27.6° S, 152.8° E

Palaeocoordinates   53.253° S, 154.107° E

Stratigraphic Information   Redbank Plains Formation, lacustrine; lithified, brown, yellow, muddy ironstone

Geological Age   Late Triassic (Norian)

Age Mya   ~227 to 208.5 Mya

Comments

Riek (1952) "In addition to the above described specimens [Isoptera; Orthoptera] there are a few fragmentary remains too indefinite for specific description. There is an almost complete hindwing of a cicada differing little from recent forms, **also a small fragment of the forewing of an anisopterous Odonata**, and finally a very small fragment doubtfully referred to as Orthopteron."

Not Determined (Mount Crosby)

Repository	Queensland Museum
Registration Number(s)	C-1536-7; C-1538-9
Reference	

Riek, E. F. (1955). Fossil insects from the Triassic beds at Mt. Crosby, Queensland. *Australian Journal of Zoology* **3**(4):654-691.

Locality	Mt Crosby Insect Bed
Geocordinates	27.6° S, 152.8° E
Palaeocoordinates	67.9° S, 125.0° E

Stratigraphic Information (from Paleobiology Database)

"at the bottom of the Ipswich Series" well below the Denmark Hill bed

Carnian according to Barone-Nugent et al. 2003. Purdy. & Cranfield (2013) reported an unpublished SHRIMP date of 226±2 Ma for the Brisbane Tuff. Therefore, the Blackstone Formation may be considered younger than 226 Ma in absolute age. Thus, the Ipswich Coal Measures above the Brisbane Tuff, which is to say, the succession from the Mount Crosby Formation to the top of the Blackstone Formation must now be considered Norian

Geological Age	Triassic: Norian
Age MYA	221.5 to 205.6 Ma
Comments	

Riek (1955) "Only two very fragmentary specimens of Odonata, C-1536-7 and C-1538-9, have so far been discovered from these beds. They are mentioned merely to indicate the presence of an odonate element in the preserved insect fauna."

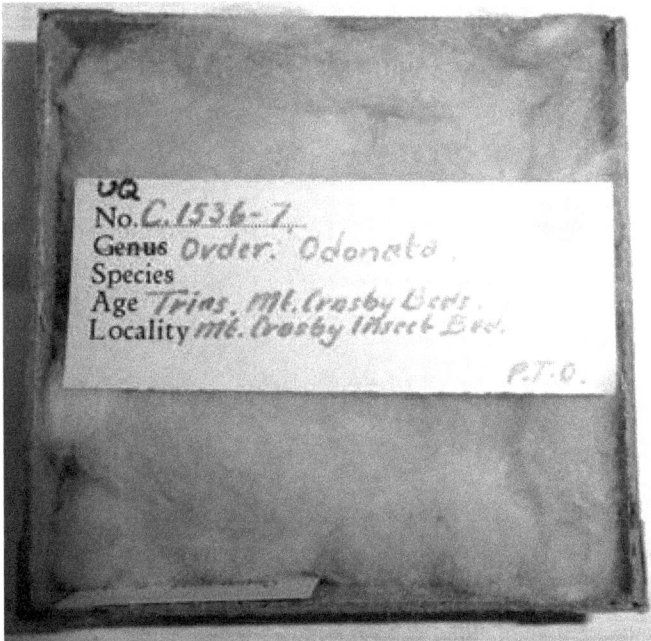

Figure 65 - C 1536-7

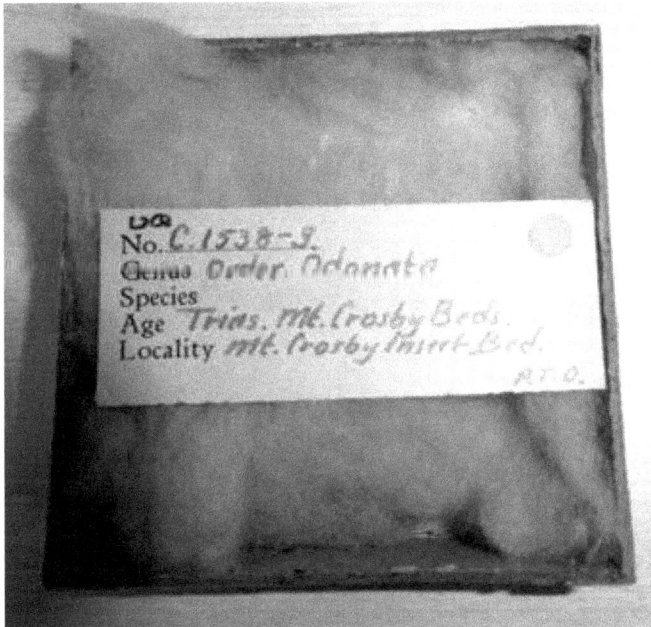

Figure 66 - C 1538-9

Not Determined (Talbragar)

Repository	Australian Museum
Registration Number(s)	F.137574
	F.137575 (counterpart)

Description

Beattie, R.G. & Avery, S. (2012). Palaeoecology and palaeoenvironment of the Jurassic Talbragar Fossil Fish Bed, Gulgong, New South Wales, Australia, *Alcheringa* 36: 453-468 [Fig 8E]

Locality - Talbragar Fossil Fish Bed, Farr's Hill, NSW

Geocordinates	32.2° S, 149.7° E
Palaeocoordinates	73.6° S, 117.8° E

Stratigraphic Information (from Paleobiology Database)_

The deposit represents a remnant of sedimentary accumulation in a freshwater lake. Sediment is largely derived from consolidated volcanic ash.

Geological Age Late Jurassic: Latest Oxfordian-Tithonian, or early Tithonian.

Although previously regarded to be of Early Jurassic age (Hind & Helby 1969), a latest Oxfordian–Tithonian (Late Jurassic) age has recently been determined by SHRIMP analysis of zircon crystals obtained from this unit (Turner et al. 2009)

Age MYA   151.55 +/- 4.27 Ma (error bar falls within Kimmeridgian).

Comments

Beattie & Avery (2012) "Odonata (immature)"

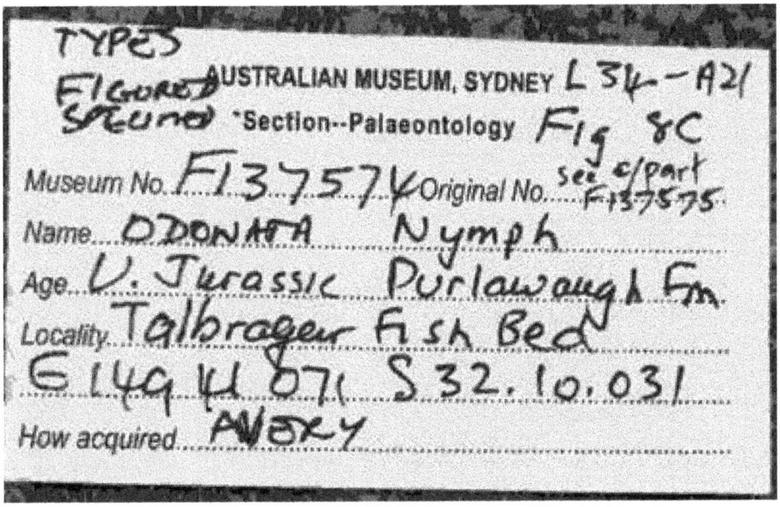

TYPES
FIGURED SPECIMEN
AUSTRALIAN MUSEUM, SYDNEY L34-A21
*Section--Palaeontology Fig 8C
Museum No. F137574 Original No. see c/part F137575
Name ODONATA Nymph
Age U. Jurassic Purlawaugh Fm
Locality Talbragar Fish Bed
E149 41 071 S32.10.031
How acquired AVERY

Figure 64 - F.137574

Aeroplana mirabilis Tillyard, 1916

Repository	QueenslandMuseum	Natural History Museum
Registration Number(s)	GSQI126a	In33396 counterpart

Original description

Tillyard, R. J. (1918). Mesozoic Insects of Queensland. No. 3 Odonata and Protodonata. *The Proceedings of the Linnean Society of New South Wales* **43**:417-436, [pp. 426-434, Text Figs. 14,15; pls 44-45]

Etymology of genus name

"Tillyard (1918: 428) "… it is clear that the wings of this insect were excessively long and narrow, being in shape not unlike the wings of a modern aeroplane. This character suggested to me the name of the genus." With a feminine ending –a.

Etymology of species name

L. *mirabilis* = wonderful strange

Locality	Denmark Hill Insect Bed, QLD
Geocordinates	27.6° S, 152.8° E
Palaeocoordinates	67.9° S, 125.0° E

Stratigraphic Information (from Paleobiology Database)

Interbedded sandstones and mudstones accumulated on levees bordering channels and graded laterally into floodplains where carbonaceous mudstones accumulated with thin crevasse splay sandstone beds.

The Insect bed is about 50 feet above the Bluff coal seam and 50 feet below the Aberdare coal seam. Fossil bed is 15 cm thick. Purdy & Cranfield (2013) reported an unpublished SHRIMP date of 226±2 Ma for the Brisbane Tuff. Therefore, the Blackstone Formation may be considered younger than 226 Ma in absolute age. Thus, the Ipswich Coal Measures above the

Brisbane Tuff, which is to say, the succession from the Mount Crosby Formation to the top of the Blackstone Formation must now be considered Norian.

Geological Age   Late Triassic: Norian

Age Mya   221.5 - 205.6 Ma

Collector & Date   Collected by Dunstan & Wilcox in 1915-1916

Voucher Number from Original Description

Tillyard (1918) "Type, Specimen No. 126a, (Coll. Queensland Geological Survey)."

Comments

Tillyard (1923) "After further study of the Order Protodonata, I am unable to admit the retension of the genus *Aeroplana* in this Order. This type of wing appears to be a highly specialised offshoot from the Palaeodictyoptera, showing some affinities with the Protorthoptera on account of the structure of the much simplified radial sector and the many-branched media. I propose, therefore, to treat the Aeroplanoptera as a distinct Order rather than as a Sub-order of the Protodonata."

Handlirsch, A. (1939:1). "Die von Tillyard als Protodonate beschriebene *Aeroplana* ist eine Stabheuschrecke". ["The *Aeroplana* described by Tillyard as Protodonata is a stick insect]

Riek (1956), following Handlirsch, classifies it as Phasmodea: Chresmododoea: Aeroplanidae, Tillyard

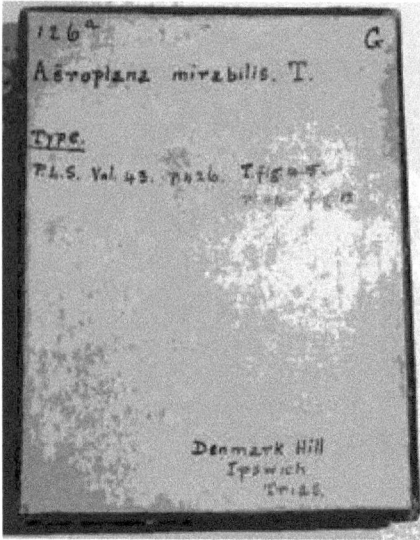

Figure 67 - GSQI126a

Figure 68 - GSQI126a

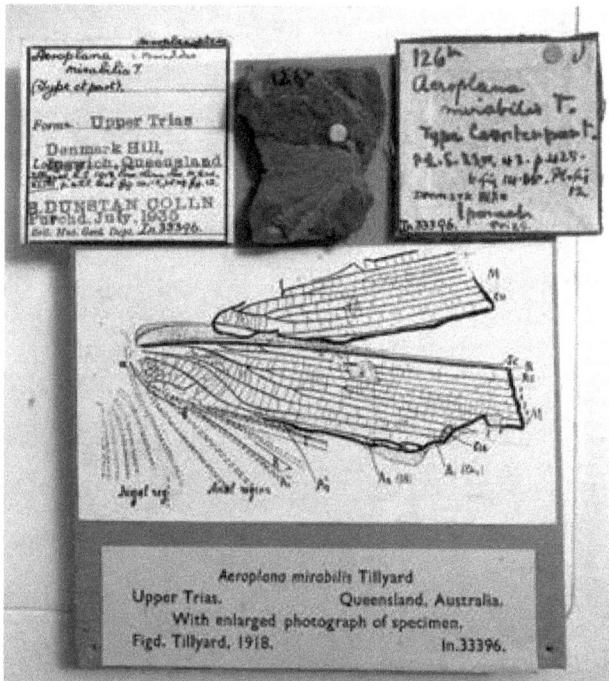

Figure 69 - In 33396 counterpart

Antitaxineura *anomala* Tillyard, 1935

Repository   Natural History Museum

Registration Number(s)   In 46392, part and counterpart

Original description

> Tillyard, R. J. (1935a). Upper Permian insects of New South Wales. IV. The order Odonata. *Proceedings of the Linnean Society of New South Wales* **60**:374-391. [pp. 382 – 384; Text fig. 4]

Etymology of genus name

> Tillyard (1935a:374) states "The known Odonate fauna of New South Wales can now be classified under … *Polytaxineura* n.g.[and] *Antitaxineura* n.g." Gr. ἀντί= opposite = τάξις = arrangement + Gr. νεῦρον = nerve, or wing veins in entomology. neura (in odonate names) = veined; the philological explanation is somewhat complicated: the element in question is the adjectival Greek morpheme –neuros = veined; but its feminine ending in Greek is –os but for nomenclature it is transferred to Latin, where the feminine form becomes –a

Etymology of species name

> Gr. ἀνώμαλος = anomalous. Perhaps the name refers to the parallel struts on either side of the nodus mentioned as peculiar (Tillyard 1953a:383) (different from *Ditaxineura* and *Polytaxineura*), .

Locality - Warner's Bay, Belmont, NSW

Geocordinates   33.0° S, 151.6° E

Palaeocoordinates   68.25° S, 145.3° E

Collector and Date   collected by T.H. Pincombe 1931

Lithological Information [from Knight (1950)]

> The rock in which the insect remains are found is a hard, very fine-grained chert about two feet six inches thick. Stratification is pronounced and well-defined joints cause the chert to break into rhomb-shaped blocks. The colour is light-grey to bluishgrey near its upper surface and becomes black towards the lower boundary.

Geological Age	Late Permian: Changhsingian
Age Mya	254.0 - 252.3 Ma

Voucher Number from Original Description

Tillyard (1935a) "Type, - *Holotype*, Specimen P 127, A and B: A, obverse impression; B, reverse impression." but repository not stated

Comments

> *Antitaxineura anomala* is recombined as *Stenoperlidium anomala* Tillyard, 1935b: 386-388 [Plecoptera: Eustheniidae] according to Jell 2004: 17

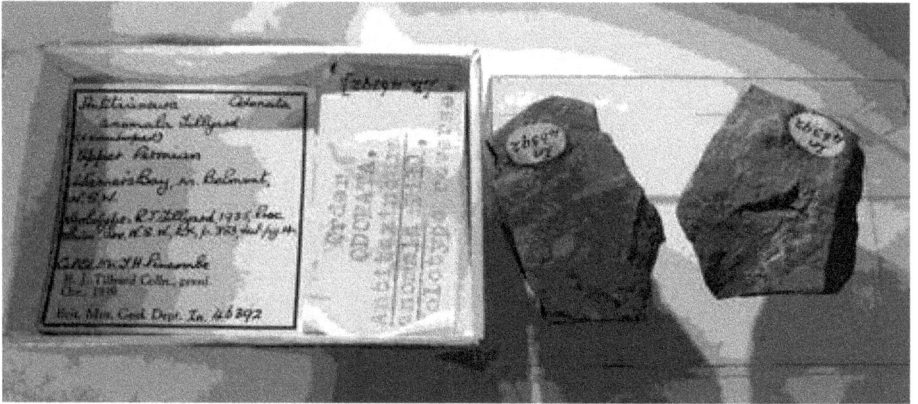

Figure 70 - In 46392 part and counterpart

Austrolestidion duaringae Tillyard, 1916

Repository	QM	Natural History Museum
Registration Number(s)	GSQ20a	In. 33297 (= BD20b, counterpar)

Original description

> Tillyard, R. J. (1916). Descriptions of the fossil Insects and stratigraphical features. *Queensland Geological Survey* (253): 11-70. [pp. 45 – 47; pl. 1, fig. 6]

Etymology of genus name

> (Tillyard 1916:47) "The length and narrowness of the gills is also an interesting point, since it shows us that *Austrolestes cingulatus*, Burm, generally regarded as the most archaic member of the genus, still possesses gills closest in form to those found on the fossil larvae." L. auster (stem austro–) = south wind, hence south + *Lestes* Gr. ληστής (= a robber or pirate + Gr. diminutive suffix –ίδιον.

Etymology of species name

> A toponym from its locality

Locality - Duaringa Core, QLD

Geocordinates	23,7° S, 149.7° E
Palaeocoordinates	44.4° S, 149.3° E

Stratigraphic Information (from Paleobiology Database)

> Its type locality is the Duaringa core, which is in an Eocene terrestrial shale in the Duaringa Formation of Australia. Cores from the bore consisted almost entirely of bluish and buff-coloured clays and shales, with occasional bands of lignite.

Geological Age	Late Eocene
Age Mya	37.2 - 33.9 Ma

Voucher Number from Original Description

Tillyard (1916) "TYPES : Specs. 20a and 20b (counterparts) (B. D. Coll.)"

Comments

Decapoda: Parastacidae according to Rozefelds (1985) "… was initially interpreted as representing two zygopteran nymphs lying obliquely across each other (Tillyard, 1916). The specimen, however, is quite heavily calcified and badly crushed and probably represents a juvenile parastacid crustacean. The 'compound eye' and two sets of 'gills' to which Tillyard referred, represent respectively parts of the uropods and the chelae of the first pereiopod."

Figure 71 - In 33297 counterpart

Mesomantidion queenslandicum Tillyard, 1916

Repository	QM	NHMUK
Registration Number(s)	GSQI1a	In33278 (counterpart)

Original description

> Tillyard, R. J. (1916). Descriptions of the fossil Insects; Mesozoic and Tertiary Insects of Queensland and New South Wales. Descriptions of the fossil Insects and stratigraphical features. *Queensland Geological Survey* (253)11-70. [pp. 16 – 17; pl. 5, fig.2]

Etymology of genus name

> Tillyard (1916:16) "It shows the very peculiar convexly curved anterior border still preserved in certain recent Mantoids," Meso (probably from Mesozoic) + Mantid + Gr. diminutive suffix – ίδιον.

Etymology of species name

> A toponym from the state in Australia in which it was found + L. suffix *–icus, –ica, –icum* = belonging to.

Locality - Ipswich Basin: Blackstone Formation: Denmark Hill Insect Bed, QLD

Geocordinates	27.6° S, 152.8° E
Palaeocoordinates	58.6° S, 101.0° E

Stratigraphic Information (from Paleobiology Database)

> Interbedded sandstones and mudstones accumulated on levees bordering channels and graded laterally into floodplains where carbonaceous mudstones accumulated with thin crevasse splay sandstone beds.

> The Insect bed is about 50 feet above the Bluff coal seam and 50 feet below the Aberdare coal seam. Fossil bed is 15 cm thick. Purdy & Cranfield (2013) reported an unpublished

SHRIMP date of 226±2 Ma for the Brisbane Tuff. Therefore, the Blackstone Formation may be considered younger than 226 Ma in absolute age. Thus, the Ipswich Coal Measures above the Brisbane Tuff, which is to say, the succession from the Mount Crosby Formation to the top of the Blackstone Formation must now be considered Norian.

Geological Age   Late Triassic: Norian

Age Mya   221.5 - 205.6 Ma

Voucher Number from Original Description

Tillyard (1916) "TYPE: Spec. 1a . TYPE-COUNTERPART : Spec. 1b. (B. D. Coll.)"

Comments

Tillyard (1916: 17) "*Mesomantidion* is nearer to a definite phylogenetic connection between the Protorthoptera and recent Mantoidea."

Riek (1956: 110) "This is not considered to be an insect, but if it is, its relationships are very problematical."

Jell (2004: 14) lists it under Odonata.

Figure 72 - GSQI1a

Figure 73 - In 33278

The Indexes

Museum Holdings   98

Fossils by Locality   102

Holotype Repository   107

MUSEUM HOLDINGS

Australian Museum, Sydney

Austrogomphus	1	McGraths Flat
Austrogomphus	2	McGraths Flat
Austrogomphus	3	McGraths Flat
Austrogomphus	4	McGraths Flat
Austrogomphus	5	McGraths Flat
Austrogomphus	6	McGraths Flat
Austrogomphus	7	McGraths Flat
Austrogomphus	8	McGraths Flat
Austrogomphus	9	McGraths Flat
Austrogomphus	10	McGraths Flat
Austrogomphus	11	McGraths Flat
Austrogomphus	12	McGraths Flat
Austrogomphus	13	McGraths Flat
Austroprotolindenia jurassica	F. 141097	Talbragar
Austroprotolindenia jurassica	F. 141098	Talbragar
Austroprotolindenia jurassica	F. 136868	Talbragar
Austroprotolindenia jurassica	F. 13869	Talbragar
Corduliidae indet	1	McGraths Flat
Corduliidae indet	2	McGraths Flat
Corduliidae indet	3	McGraths Flat
Meganisoptera	F. 43142	Warner's Bay

Meganisoptera	F. 43141	Warner's Bay
Mesophlebia antinodalis	F. 39270 (para)	Denmark Hill
not determined	F. 137574;	Talbragar
not determined	F. 137575	Talbragar
not determined	F. 39175	Unknown but from Tillyard collection
Triassagrion australiense	F. 39253	Denmark Hill
Triassolestes epiophlebioides	F. 39266	Denmark Hill
Triassolestes epiophlebioides	In 33469	Denmark Hill
Triassophlebia stigmatica	F. 39267	Denmark Hill

National Museum of Victoria

Coenagrionidae indet.	NMVP 103019	Koonwarra
Coenagrionidae indet.	NMVP 102510	Koonwarra
Coenagrionidae indet.	NMVP 103047	Koonwarra
Coenagrionidae indet.	NMVP 103211	Koonwarra
Coenagrionidae indet.	NMVP 123054 (was MUGD 3738)	Koonwarra
Coenagrionidae indet.	NMVP 27039	Koonwarra
Coenagrionidae indet.	NMVP 102508	Koonwarra
Coenagrionidae indet.	NMVP 102508 CP	Koonwarra
Coenagrionidae indet.	NMVP 102509	Koonwarra
Coenagrionidae indet.	NMVP 102509 CP	Koonwarra
Niwratia elongata	NMVP 102517	Koonwarra
Peraphlebia tetrastichia	NMVP 103212	Koonwarra
Peraphlebia tetrastichia	NMVP 102518A	Koonwarra
Peraphlebia tetrastichia	NMVP 123050A (was MUGD 3731A)	Koonwarra
Peraphlebia tetrastichia	NMVP 123050B (was MUGD 3731B)	Koonwarra

Natural History Museum London

[*Aeroplana mirabilis*]	In 33396 CP	Denmark Hill
Aeschnidiopsis flindersiensis	In 64602	Pelican Bore
[*Antitaxineura anomala*]	In 46392	Warner's Bay
[*Antitaxineura anomala*]	In 46392 CP	Warner's Bay
[*Austrolestidion duaringae*]	In 33297	Duaringa Core
[*Mesomantidion queenslandicum*]	In 33278	Denmark Hill
Mesophlebia antinodalis	In 33279	Denmark Hill
Mesophlebia antinodalis	In 33397	Denmark Hill
Mesophlebia antinodalis	In 33397	Denmark Hill
not determined	In 46116	Beacon Hill
not determined	In 46112	Beacon Hill
Perrisophlebia multiseriata	In 33467	Denmark Hill
Polytaxineura stanleyi	In 45781	Warner's Bay
Polytaxineura stanleyi	In 45360	Warner's Bay
Polytaxineura stanleyi	In 46395	Warner's Bay
Polytaxineura stanleyi	In 46395 CP	Warner's Bay
Samaroblatta intercalata(?)	In 33519	Denmark Hill
Tillyardomyrmeleon petermilleri	In 46119	Beacon Hill
Triassagrion australiense	In 32972	Denmark Hill
Triassagrion australiense	In 32925	Denmark Hill
Triassagrion australiense	In 32925 CP	Denmark Hill
Triassagrion australiense	In 33126	Denmark Hill
Triassagrion australiense	In 33126 CP	Denmark Hill
Triassagrion australiense	In 33226	Denmark Hill
Triassagrion australiense	In 33226 CP	Denmark Hill
Triassagrion australiense	In 33544 CP	Denmark Hill
Triassophlebia stigmatica	In 33352	Denmark Hill

Queensland Museum, Brisbane

[*Aeroplana mirabilis*]	GSQI126	Denmark Hill
Aeschna flindersiensis	GSQ368	Flinders River
Aeschnidiopsis flindersiensis	UQF.3162	Flinders River
Aeschnidiopsis flindersiensis	QMF.2421	Flinders River
Aeschnidiopsis flindersiensis	QMF.12035	Pelican Bore
Aeschnidiopsis flindersiensis	QMF44309	Winton
Aeschnidiopsis flindersiensis		Winton
[*Austrolestidion duaringae*]	GSQ20a	Duaringa Core
[*Mesomantidion queenslandicum*]	GSQI1a	Denmark Hill
Mesophlebia antinodalis	GSQ 3a	Denmark Hill
Mesophlebia antinodalis	QMF 58847	Wondai
not determined	C-1536-7	Mt Crosby
not determined	C-1538-9	Mt Crosby
Perrisophlebia multiseriata	QGS203	Denmark Hill
Samarura	QMF 12996a	Brassall Quarry
Samarura	QMF 12996b	Brassall Quarry

Fossils By Locality

Beacon Hill, Brookvale, near Manly, NSW

not determined	In 46116	NHMUK
not determined	In 46112	NHMUK
Tillyardomyrmeleon petermilleri	In 46119	NHMUK

Brassall Quarry, QLD

Samarura	QMF 12996a	QM
Samarura	QMF 12996b	QM

Denmark Hill Insect Bed, QLD

[*Aeroplana mirabilis*]	In 33396 CP	NHMUK
[*Aeroplana mirabilis*]	GSQI126	QM
[*Mesomantidion queenslandicum*]	In 33278	NHMUK
[*Mesomantidion queenslandicum*]	GSQI1a	QM
Mesophlebia antinodalis	F. 39270 (para)	AM
Mesophlebia antinodalis	In 33279	NHMUK
Mesophlebia antinodalis	In 33397 Tierney	NHMUK
Mesophlebia antinodalis	In 33397 Tierney	NHMUK
Mesophlebia antinodalis	GSQ 3a	QM
Perrisophlebia multiseriata	In 33467	NHMUK
Perrisophlebia multiseriata	QGS203	QM
Samaroblatta intercalata (?)	In 33519	NHMUK
Triassagrion australiense	F. 39253	AM

Triassagrion australiense	In 32972	NHMUK
Triassagrion australiense	In 32925	NHMUK
Triassagrion australiense	In 32925 CP	NHMUK
Triassagrion australiense	In 33126	NHMUK
Triassagrion australiense	In 33126 CP	NHMUK
Triassagrion australiense	In 33226	NHMUK
Triassagrion australiense	In 33226 CP	NHMUK
Triassagrion australiense	In 33544 CP	NHMUK
Triassolestes epiophlebioides	F. 39266	AM
Triassolestes epiophlebioides	In 33469	NHMUK
Triassophlebia stigmatica	F. 39267	AM
Triassophlebia stigmatica	In 33352	NHMUK

Duaringa Core, QLD

[*Austrolestidion duaringae*]	In. 33297	NHMUK
[*Austrolestidion duaringae*]	GSQ20a	QM

Flinders River Beds, QLD

Aeschna flindersiensis	GSQ368	QM
Aeschnidiopsis flindersiensis	UQF.3162	QM
Aeschnidiopsis flindersiensis	QMF.2421	QM

Koonwarra Fossil Bed, VIC

Coenagrionidae indet.	NMVP 103019	NMV
Coenagrionidae indet.	NMVP 102510	NMV
Coenagrionidae indet.	NMVP 103047	NMV
Coenagrionidae indet.	NMVP 103211	NMV

Coenagrionidae indet.	NMVP 123054 (was MUGD 3738)	NMV
Coenagrionidae indet.	NMVP 27039	NMV
Coenagrionidae indet.	NMVP 102508	NMV
Coenagrionidae indet.	NMVP 102508 CP	NMV
Coenagrionidae indet.	NMVP 102509	NMV
Coenagrionidae indet.	NMVP 102509 CP	NMV
Niwratia elongata	NMVP 102517	NMV
Peraphlebia tetrastichia	NMVP 103212	NMV
Peraphlebia tetrastichia	NMVP 102518A	NMV
Peraphlebia tetrastichia	NMVP 123050A (was MUGD 3731A)	NMV
Peraphlebia tetrastichia	NMVP 123050B (was MUGD 3731B)	NMV

McGraths Flat, NSW

Austrogomphus	1	AM
Austrogomphus	2	AM
Austrogomphus	3	AM
Austrogomphus	4	AM
Austrogomphus	5	AM
Austrogomphus	6	AM
Austrogomphus	7	AM
Austrogomphus	8	AM
Austrogomphus	9	AM
Austrogomphus	10	AM
Austrogomphus	11	AM
Austrogomphus	12	AM
Austrogomphus	13	AM
Corduliidae indet	1	AM
Corduliidae indet	2	AM
Corduliidae indet	3	AM

Mt Crosby Insect Bed, QLD

not determined	C-1536-7	QM
not determined	C-1538-9	QM

Pelican Bore, QLD

Aeschnidiopsis flindersiensis	QMF.12035	QM
Aeschnidiopsis flindersiensis	In 64602	NHMUK

Talbragar Fossil Fish Bed, Farr's Hill, NSW

Austroprotolindenia jurassica	F. 141097	AM
Austroprotolindenia jurassica	F. 141098	AM
Austroprotolindenia jurassica	F. 136868	AM
Austroprotolindenia jurassica	F. 13869	AM
not determined	F. 137574;	AM
not determined	F. 137575	AM

Unknown, but from Tillyard Collection

not determined	F. 39175	AM

Warner's Bay, Belmont, NSW

Antitaxineura anomala	In 46392	NHMUK
Antitaxineura anomala	In 46392 CP	NHMUK
Meganisoptera	F. 43142	AM
Meganisoptera	F. 43141	AM
Polytaxineura stanleyi	In 45781	NHMUK
Polytaxineura stanleyi	In 45360	NHMUK

| *Polytaxineura stanleyi* | In 46395 (p&cp) | NHMUK |
| *Polytaxineura stanleyi* | In 46395 CP | NHMUK |

Winton, QLD

| *Aeschnidiopsis flindersiensis* | QMF44309 | QM |
| *Aeschnidiopsis flindersiensis* | counterpart | QM |

Wondai, QLD

| *Mesophlebia antinodalis* | QMF 58847 | QM |

Holotype Repository

[*Aeroplana mirabilis*]	GSQI126	QM	Denmark Hill
Aeschnidiopsis flindersiensis	GSQ368	QM	Flinders River
[*Antitaxineura anomala*]	In 46392	NHMUK	Warner's Bay
[*Austrolestidion duaringae*]	GSQ20	QM	Duaringa Core
Austroprotolindenia jurassica	F. 136868	AM	Talbragar
[*Mesomantidion queenslandicum*]	GSQI1a	QM	Denmark Hill
Mesophlebia antinodalis	GSQ 3a	QM	Denmark Hill
Niwratia elongata	NMVP 102517	NMV	Koonwarra
Peraphlebia tetrastichia	NMVP 103212	NMV	Koonwarra
Peraphlebia tetrastichia	NMVP 123050B (was MUGD 3731B)	NMV	Koonwarra
Perrisophlebia multiseriata	QGS203	QM	Denmark Hill
Polytaxineura stanleyi	In 46395	NHMUK	Warner's Bay
Tillyardomyrmeleon petermilleri	In 46119	NHMUK	Beacon Hill
Triassagrion australiense	F. 39253	AM	Denmark Hill
Triassolestes epiophlebioides	F. 39266	AM	Denmark Hill
Triassophlebia stigmatica	F. 39267	AM	Denmark Hill

Acknowledgements

Matthew Mc Curry, Patrick Smith (Australian Museum);

Andrew Rozefelds, Kirsten Spring, Professor Alan Rix [with especial thanks for his valued discussions] (Queensland Museum);

Rolf Schmidt (Melbourne Museum)

Claire Mellish, Lil Stevens, Jenny Parry (London Natural History Museum);

Gavin Dally (MAGNT Darwin);

Adamm Yates (MAGNT Alice Spring);

Sarah Martin, Mikael Siversson (Western Australian Museum);

Mary-Anne Binnie (South Australian Museum);

Dr Heinrich Fliedner gave invaluable help with the etymologies.

Dr Stephen Poropat (Swinburne University) who advised that a dragonfly fossil had been found at Winton; who supervised the Honours Project of Elaine Anderson which confirmed *Niwratia elongata* was an odonate larva; and summarised most of the fossil specimens known from Australian museums.

Trish Sloan (Australian Age of Dinosaurs Museum of Natural History)

Dr. Johan Renaudie (Museum für Naturkunde in Berlin) kindly produced the palaeocoordinates and palaeomaps using Gplates.

Dr. Benjamin Kear (Museum of Evolution Uppsala University) provided the map of Australian Mesozoic deposits.

Dr. Viktor Baranov (Ludwig-Maximilians-Universität Munich Biocenter, Department of Biology) for information about the McGraths Flat Miocene deposit.

Stratigraphic, lithological and some collector information was extracted from The Paleobiology Database (PBDB) under a CC BY 4.0 International License.

The frontispiece was produced using Dmap.

Figure Credits

Elaine Anderson – 8, 9, 14, 15, 17, 18, 19, 21, 22, 24, 25, 26, 29, 35, 36, 37, 38, 39, 40, 41, 42, 47, 48, 72; Australian Age of Dinosaurs – 13;

Ian Endersby – 3, 4, 5, 6, 7, 16, 27, 28, 31, 32, 34, 50, 56, 58, 59, 64, 65, 66, 67, 68

Benjamin Kear – 1;

Alan Rix – 10, 12;

Royal Society of Queensland, Proceedings – 2;

Andrew Rozefelds – 2;

Rolf Schmidt – 23; Lil Stevens – 11, 30, 33, 43, 44, 45 49, 51, 52, 53, 54, 55, 57, 60, 61, 62, 63, 70, 71, 73.

References

Anderson, E. (2018). *Cretaceous Odonata from the Koonwarra Lagerstätte, Victoria, Australia.* B.Sc. Hons) Thesis, Swinburne University of Technology, Melbourne.

BARONE-NUGENT, E.D., McLOUGHLIN, S. & DRINNAN, A.N. (2003). New species of *Rochipteris* from the Upper Triassic of Australia. *Review of Palaeobotany and Palynology* **123**: 273-287

Barth, G., Nel, A. & Franz, M. (2013). Two new odonate-like insect wings from the latest Norian of northern Germany. *Polskie Pismo Entomologiczne* [Polish Journal of Entomology] **82**: 127-142

Bean, L.B. (2006). The leptolepid fish *Cavenderichthys talbragarensis* (Woodward, 1895) from the Talbragar Fish Bed (Late Jurassic) near Gulgong, New South Wales. *Records of the Western Australian Museum* **23**: 43–76.

Beattie, R.G. & Avery, S. (2012). Palaeoecology and palaeoenvironment of the Jurassic Talbragar Fossil Fish Bed, Gulgong, New South Wales, Australia, *Alcheringa* **36**: 453-468.

Beattie, R. G. & Nel, A. (2012). A new dragonfly, *Austroprotolindenia jurassica* (Odonata: Anisoptera), from the Upper Jurassic of Australia. *Alcheringa* **36**:189-193. [pp. 2-3; figs. 1, 2]

Bechly, G., 1996. Morphologische Untersuchungen am Flügelgeäder der rezenten Libellen und deren Stammgruppenvertreter (Insecta: Pterygota, Odonata), unter besonderer Berücksichtigung der Phylogenetischen Systematik und der Grundplanes der *Odonata. *Petalura* special volume2, 1–402 (revised edition of the previous publication, with an English appendix including a new phylogenetic system of fossil and extant odonates).

Bechly, G., (1997). New fossil Odonata from the Upper Triassic of Italy, with a redescription of *Italophlebia gervasutti*, and a reclassification of Triassic dragonflies. *Rivista del Museo Civico di Scienze Naturale E. Caffi* **19**: 31–70.

Burns, A.N., 1955. Rediscovery of a "living fossil" damsel-fly in Victoria. *Victorian. Naturalist* **72**: 116-117.

Brauer, F., Redtenbacher, J. & Ganglbauer, L. (1889). Fossile Insekten aus der Juraformation Ost-Sibiriens. *Mémoires de l'Académie Impériale des Sciences de St.-Pétersbourg*, VII Série **36**(15):1-22. [pp. 7 – 9; figs. 6 – 10.

Calvert, P.P. (1903). Entomological Literature [review]. *Entomological News* **14**(6): 208-209

Carpenter F. M. (1992) , *Treatise on Invertebrate Paleontology* Part R, Arthropoda 4: Superclass Hexapoda 3/4, 1-655.

Cowley, J. (1942). Descriptions of some genera of fossil Odonata. *Proceedings of the Royal Entomological Society of London. Series B, Taxonomy* **11**:63-7.

Drinnan, A.N. & Chambers, T.C. (1986). Flora of the Lower Cretaceous Koonwarra Fossil Bed (Korumburra Group), South Gippsland, Victoria (Australia) pp. 1-77 in. Plants and invertebrates from the Lower Cretaceous Koonwarra Fossil Bed, South Gippsland, Victoria. (ed. Jell, P.A. & Roberts, J.) Association of Australasian Palaeontologists: Sydney.

Elliott, D. & Cook. A. (2004). Black Soil: a bug's life. *Australian Age of Dinosaurs Journal* **2**: 13.

Fleck G., Nel A. (2003) Revision of the Mesozoic family Aeschnidiidae (Odonata: Anisoptera), *Zoologica* **153**: 1-170.

Fletcher, H.O. (1971). Catalogue of type specimens in the Australian Museum, Sydney. *Australian Museum Memoirs* **13**: 1–167.

Grimaldi, D. & Engel, M.S. (2005). *Evolution of the Insects*. Cambridge University Press: Cambridge.

Handlirsch A. (1908) Die fossilen Insekten und die Phylogenie der rezenten Formen. (bound volume of part work, this vol. includes Parts I, II, III. Verlag Wilhelm Engelmann, Leipzig 1-672 + plates.

Handlirsch, A. (1939). Neue Untersuchungen über die fossilen Insekten mit Ergänzungen und Nachträgen sowie Ausblicken auf phylogenetische, palaeogeographische und allgemein biologische Probleme. *Annalen des Naturhistorischen Museums in Wien* **49**: 1 – 240.

Henrotay, M.; Nel, A.; Jarzembowski, E.A., (1997). New protomyrmeleontid damselflies from the Triassic of Australia and the Liassic of Luxembourg, with the description of *Tillyardomyrmeleon petermilleri* gen. nov. and spec. nov. Archizygoptera: Protomyrmeleontidae. *Odonatologica* **26**(4): 395-404. [pp. 396 - 397; fig. 1].

Huang, D-Y.. (2015). *Tarwinia australis* (Siphonaptera: Tarwiniidae) from the Lower Cretaceous Koonwarra fossil bed: Morphological revision and analysis of its evolutionary relationship. *Cretaceous Research*: **52**: 507-515.

Huguet A., Nel A., Martinez-Delclos X., Bechly G. & Martins-Neto, R. (2002) Preliminary phylogenetic analysis of the Protanisoptera (Insecta: Odonatoptera) *Geobios* **35**: 537-560.

Jell P. A. (1993) Late Triassic homopterous nymph from Dinmore, Ipswich Basin, *Memoirs of the Queensland Museum* **33**: 360.

Jell, P. (2004). The fossil insects of Australia. *Memoirs of the Queensland Museum* **50**:1-124.

Jell, P. A. & Duncan, P. M. (1986). Invertebrates, mainly insects, from the freshwater, Lower Cretaceous, Koonwarra Fossil Bed (Korumburra Group), South Gippsland, Victoria. *Memoirs of the Association of Australasian Palaeontologists* **3**:111-205. [pp. 126-131; figs. 8-10].

Kear, B. P., & Hamilton-Bruce, R.-J. (2011). *Dinosaurs in Australia: Mesozoic Life from the Southern Continent*. CSIRO Publishing.

Knight, O. Le M. (1950). Fossil insect beds of Belmont, N.S.W. *Records of the Australian Museum* **22**(3): 251–253.

Lewis, C.T. & Short, C. (1963) *Latin Dictionary Based on Andrews's edition of Freund's Latin Dictionary*. Oxford University Press: New York. xiv 2018 pp.

Liddell, H.G. & Scott, R. (1996) *A Greek Lexicon*. 9th ed with a revised supplement. Clarendon Press: Oxford. xlv 2042 pp. Supplement xxxi 320 pp.

Mather, P. (1986) *A Time for a Museum : History of the Queensland Museum 1826-1986* Queensland Museum: Brisbane.

McCurry, M.R., Cantrill, D.J., Smith, P.M., Beattie, R., Dettmann, M. Baranov, V., Magee, C., Nguyen. J.M.T., Forster, M.A., Hinde. J., Pogson, R., Wang, H., Marjo, C.E., Vasconcelos, P. & Michael Frese, M. (2022). A Lagerstätte from Australia provides insight into the nature of Miocene mesic ecosystems. *Science Advances* 8 eabm 1406, 07 Jan 2022: 11 pp.

Nel, A., Frese, M., McLean, G. & Beattie, R. (2017). A forewing of the Jurassic dragonfly *Austroprotolindenia jurassica* Beattie & Nel (Odonata: Anisoptera) from the Talbragar Fish Bed, New South Wales, Australia, *Alcheringa*: **41**, 532-535.

Nel, A., Marie, V., & Schmeißner, S. (2002). Revision of the Lower Mesozoic dragonfly family Triassolestidae Tillyard, 1918 (Odonata: Epiproctophora). *Annales de Paléontologie* **88**:189-214.

Nel, A. & Martínez-Delclòs, X. (1993): Essai de Révision des Aeschnidioidea (Insecta, Odonata, Anisoptera). — C.N.R.S. Editions. Paris. *Cahiers de Paléontologie*: 1–99, 52 text-figs.

Nel, A. & Paicheler, J. C. (1994). Les Libelluloidea autres que Libellulidae fossiles Un inventaire critique (Odonata, Corduliidae, Macromiidae, Synthemistidae, Chlorogomphidae et Mesophlebiidae). *Nouvelle Revue d'Entomologie* **11**:321-334.

Nel, A., Petrulevicius, J.F. & Martínez-Delclòs, X. (2005). New Mesozoic Protomyrmeleontidae (Insecta: Odonaptera: Archizygoptera) from Asia with a new phylogenetic analysis. *Journal of Systematic Palaeontology* **3** (2): 187-201.

Parfrey, S.M. (1996). Geological Survey of Queensland Fossil Collection: Catalogue of type, figured and cited fossils. https://geoscience.data.qld.gov.au/data/report/cr088740

Pole, M. (2019). Early Eocene plant macrofossils from the Booval Basin, Dinmore, near Brisbane, Queensland. *Palaeontologica Electronica* https://palaeo-electronica.org/content/2019/2760-dinmore-plant-macrofossil

Pritykina, L.N. (1981). New Triassic Odonata of middle Asia. In: Vishniakova, V.N., Dlussky, G.M., Pritykina, L.N. (Eds.), *New Insects from the Territory of the U.S.S.R.* Trudy Paleontologiceskogo Instituta Akademii nauk S.S.S.R, Moscow, 183, pp. 5–42 (in Russian).

Purdy, D.J. & Cranfield, L.C. 2013. Ipswich Basin. Pp 391–396. In Jell, P.A. (ed.) *Geology of Queensland*. (Geological Survey of Queensland: [Brisbane]).

Riek, E. F. (1952). Fossil insects from the Tertiary sediments at Dinmore, Queensland. *University of Queensland Papers, Department of Geology* 4: 17-22, pl. 1.

Riek, E. F. (1954). A second specimen of the dragon-fly *Aeschnidiopsis flindersiensis* (Woodward) from the Queensland Cretaceous. *The Proceedings of the Linnean Society of New South Wales* **79**:61-62.

Riek, E. F. (1955). Fossil insects from the Triassic beds at Mt. Crosby, Queensland. *Australian Journal of Zoology* **3**(4):654-691.

Riek, E. F. (1956). A re-examination of the mecopteroid and orthopteroid fossils (Insecta) from the Triassic beds at Denmark Hill, Queensland, with descriptions of further specimens. *Australian Journal of Zoology* **4**:98-110.

Riek, E. F. (1968). Undescribed fossil insects from the Upper Permian of Belmont, New South Wales (with an appendix listing the described species). *Records of the Australian Museum* **27**(15): 303–310.

Riek, E. F. (1970). Lower Cretaceous Fleas. *Nature* **227**: 746–747.

Rix, A. (2021). The Triassic insects of Denmark Hill, Ipswich, Southeast Queensland: the creation, use and dispersal of a collection. *Memoirs of the Queensland Museum – Nature* **62**: 217–242.

Rozefelds, A. C. (1985). A Fossil Zygopteran Nymph (Insecta: Odonata) from the Late Triassic Aberdare Conglomerate: Southeast Queensland. *Proceedings of the Royal Society of Queensland* **96**:25-32.

Thomas J.A., Trueman J.W.,Rambaut A. & Welch J.J. (2013). Relaxed phylogenetics and the Palaeoptera problem: resolving deep ancestral splits in the insect phylogeny. *Systematic Biology.* **62**: 285-297.

Tierney, A., Deregnaucourt, I., Anderson, J.M., Tierney, P. Wappler, T. & Béthoux, O. (2020): The *Triassic Mesophlebiidae*, a little closer to the crown of the Odonata (Insecta) than other 'triassolestids'. *Alcheringa*: **44**:2, 279-285.

Tillyard, R. J. (1916). Descriptions of the fossil Insects; Mesozoic and Tertiary Insects of Queensland and New South Wales. Descriptions of the fossil Insects and stratigraphical features. *Queensland Geological Survey* (253)11-70. [pp. 16 – 17; pl. 5, fig.2] [pp. 25-26; pl. 4, fig.2] [pp. 45 – 47; pl. 1, fig. 6]

Tillyard, R. J. (1917). Mesozoic Insects of Queensland no. 2 The fossil dragonfly *Aeschnidiopsis* (*Aeschna*) *flindersiensis* Woodward, from the Rolling Downs (Cretaceous) Series. *The Proceedings of the Linnean Society of New South Wales* **42**:676-692 [pls. xlii, xliii]

Tillyard, R. J. (1918). Mesozoic Insects of Queensland. No. 3 Odonata and Protodonata. *The Proceedings of the Linnean Society of New South Wales* **43**:417-436 [pp. 419-422; text figs. 11, 12b] .[pp. 424   425, text fig 13] [pp. 426-434, Text Figs. 14,15; pls 44-45]

Tillyard, R. J. (1922). Mesozoic Insects of Queensland. No. 9 Orthoptera, and additions to the Protorthoptera, Odonata, Hemiptera and Planipennia. *The Proceedings of the Linnean Society of New South Wales* **47**:447-470. [pp. 456 – 458; pl. li, fig.31; text fig. 77] [p. 454; text fig. 76]

Tillyard, R.J. (1923). Mesozoic Insects of Queensland No. 10 Summary of the Upper Iriassic insect fauna of Ipswich, Q. (Withan appendix describing new Hemiptera and Plannipennia). *Proceedings of the Linnean Society of New South Wales* **48**: 481-498.

Tillyard, R. J. (1935a). Upper Permian insects of New South Wales. IV. The order Odonata. *Proceedings of the Linnean Society of New South Wales* **60**:374-391. [pp. 383 – 384; Text fig. 4] [pp. 376-379; pl. xii, figs 1 – 3; text figs. 1 – 3]

Tillyard, R. J. (1935b). Upper Permian insects of New South Wales. V. The order Perlaria or Stone-flies. *Proceedings of the Linnean Society of New South Wales* **60**:374-391. [pp. 385– 391] [pp. 376-379; pl. xii, figs 1 – 3]

Turner S, Bean, LB, Dettmann, M, McKellar JL, McLoughlin S, & Thulborn T (2009). Australian Jurassic sedimentary and fossil successions: current work and future prospects for marine and non-marine correlation *Geologiska föreningen*:**131**(1–2): 49–70.

Wade, R.T. (1935). *The Triassic Fishes of Brookvale*, New South Wales. British Museum (Natural History): London

Whitehouse, J. (2016).Beacon Hill Shale Quarry Sydney, New South Wales, Australia:Geologic insights into its strikingly preserved Triassic fossil assemblage https://www.academia.edu/es/24223101/Beacon_Hill_shale_quarry_Sydney_New_South_Wales_Australia_Geologic_insights_into_its_strikingly_preserved_Triassic_fossil_assemblage

Woodward, H. (1884). On the wing of a neuropterous insect from the Cretaceous limestone of Flinders River, north Queensland, Australia. *Geological Magazine, Decade III* **1**:337-339 [Pl.XI Fig. 1]

Zessin, W. (1991). Die Phylogenie der Protomyrmeleontidae unter einbeziehung neuer Oberliassischer funde (Odonata: Archizygoptera sens. nov.)[Phylogeny of the Protomyrmeleontidae, with the description of new Upper Liassic material (Odonata: Archizygoptera sens. nov.)]. *Odonatologica* **20**(1):97-126.

Zherikhin, VV (2002), *Ecological history of the terrestrial insects*, pp. 331 – 387 in Rasnytsyn, A.P. & Quicke, DLJ [eds.], History of Insects. Kluwer Academic Press.

www.ingramcontent.com/pod-product-compliance
Lightning Source LLC
Chambersburg PA
CBHW052022030426

42335CB00026B/3256